FRESH AIR AND FUN

THE STORY OF A BLACKPOOL HOLIDAY CAMP

FRESH AIR AND FUN
The Story of a Blackpool Holiday Camp

by Bertha Wood

Edited by Jason Wood

With an historical introduction by John K Walton

There's a famous seaside place called Blackpool,
That's noted for fresh air and fun ...

The opening lines from 'The Lion and Albert'
by Marriott Edgar (1932).

Text copyright © Bertha Wood, 2005
Historical introduction copyright © John K. Walton, 2005

First published in 2005
by Palatine Books,
an imprint of Carnegie Publishing Ltd
Carnegie House,
Chatsworth Road,
Lancaster, LA1 4SL
www.carnegiepublishing.com

British Library Cataloguing-in-Publication data
A catalogue record for this book is available from the British Library

ISBN 10: 1-874181-36-5
ISBN 13: 978-1-874181-36-1

Designed and typeset by Carnegie Publishing
Printed and bound in the UK by Alden Press, Oxford

Contents

Bertha Wood at Ivy House about 1940, photographed by Fred.

Preface

On 20 June 2005, my grandmother, Bertha Wood, is 100 years old. 2005 also marks the 25th anniversary of the death of her husband, Fred, and the 70th anniversary of Fred and Bertha's move to Blackpool to set up the Ivy House Holiday Camp. This book, published to coincide with Bertha's centennial, is based on her memoirs which she began to write about ten years ago, even learning to master a computer.

It starts with her early life in Bolton as the daughter of a mill manager and her first steps into work in the printing and advertising trades. It was here in Bolton where she met and married Fred and their first two children were born. But then came the Great Depression and Fred's firm went into liquidation. It was at this point that Fred and Bertha's tale of enterprise and innovation really began, with a move to a new home and business in Blackpool, initially based on bed-and-breakfast lettings and market gardening, but soon flourishing as the holiday camp idea took hold. Relatively unimpeded by the war years the business went from strength to strength. A third child was born and the extended family of staff and helpers grew. Bertha treats us to descriptions of life, work and general tomfoolery in the camp, both in and out of season, including the weekly programme of participatory events, shows and concerts. Further developments at the camp and subsidiary businesses in Ilkley and Bowness are also described, as are Fred and Bertha's other interests, especially painting.

In editing Bertha's Memoirs, I have tried to be as faithful to her original words as possible. Inevitably, some rewriting and reordering has been necessary, with the main concentration being on the early years of her life and the creation and development of the camp, especially its heyday in the 1940s and 1950s. With Bertha's agreement, the later years of her life and family have not been included, save for a brief mention at the end of the book to bring her story up to date.

Interspersed throughout I have introduced a number of text panels. These are intended to provide background information or additional comments on certain subjects to help amplify the main text. Much of this material is based on discussions with surviving members of the family, friends, staff and visitors. In this respect I am very grateful to the following for sharing their own reminiscences: Peter Beighton, Mary Chamberlain, Tommy Eccles, Ron Firth, Ted Hinchcliffe, Alan Laycock, Yvonne Mantle (née Miles), Bill Poole, Jane Webster (née Throup), Frankie Whitaker, and my mother Elizabeth Wood.

As well as these discussions, one of the great pleasures of this project was the sourcing and selecting of the illustrations, ably assisted by my daughter Ellie. I should like to thank the following for the loan of material and for kindly allowing it to be reproduced in this volume: Bertha herself, Mary Chamberlain, Ron Firth, Yvonne Mantle, Johnny Smyth, Jane Webster, Frankie Whitaker, and Elizabeth Wood. Other illustrations are reproduced courtesy of Blackpool Central Library, English Heritage (National Monuments Record), and The Gazette, Blackpool. The map is reproduced from the Ordnance Survey mapping with the permission of the Controller of Her Majesty's Stationery Office.

Finally, I am extremely grateful to my friend John Walton for his initial encouragement and help with this project and for providing such an excellent historical introduction. Thanks are also due to Jimmy Perry and David Croft, and to Colin Ward, for reading the text in draft and supplying the comments reproduced on the cover. That the book appeared at all, and on time for Bertha's 100th birthday party, is due to the patience and dedication of all at Carnegie Publishing.

Jason Wood
Director
Heritage Consultancy Services

Historical introduction, by John K. Walton

From Bolton to Blackpool: a tale of enterprise and innovation

When Fred and Bertha Wood left Bolton for Blackpool in 1935, they joined a large number of refugees from the old-established industrial areas of Britain in seeking better fortune and a new life in what appeared to be the hospitable environment of the seaside. This applied especially to people from the 'cotton towns' of industrial south and east Lancashire. This area had been the seed-bed of the world's first Industrial Revolution in the late eighteenth and early nineteenth century; the centre of the 'first industrial society', overwhelmingly urban and dominated by factories, through the nineteenth century and into the twentieth; and the forcing-house for the world's first working-class consumer society around the turn of those centuries, with the development of arresting new phenomena such as the leisure industries (this is where the music-hall really began), professional spectator sport (especially football), convenience foods (pies and pastries as well as fish and chips), and popular music making (brass bands, sheet music, the piano as an item of working-class domestic furniture).[1] When hard times arrived for many industrial workers (and, as in the case of Fred and Bertha, those who provided services for the economy that employed them) after the First World War, and especially when the depression deepened in the early 1930s, trying to make a new life in Blackpool was an obvious alternative to sitting out the bad times at home and waiting for an upturn that might never come.

This applied particularly to Fred and Bertha and the many who resembled them: inventive, resourceful and optimistic people, who had already tasted some of the fruits of the new consumerism and wanted to continue to enjoy them, while providing opportunities for their children and remaining within reach of whatever help and mutual support their families and established friendship networks could provide. Viewed from Bolton, Blackpool was familiar and accessible, but different and exciting. It offered a wider range of opportunities than Bolton ever could, now that the heroic age of the unprecedented growth of the cotton industry was past. From its earliest days of rapid growth in the 1840s and 1850s, Blackpool had attracted industrial workers who wanted to risk their savings in small businesses, especially accommodation and shop-keeping; and in the difficult times of the 1920s and 1930s it became an irresistible lure for enterprising (as well as struggling and desperate) people, from the depressed Lancashire cotton towns and far beyond.[2]

Bolton

Bolton and Blackpool experienced contrasting fortunes in the interwar years. Bolton was, above all, a centre of the cotton spinning and textile engineering industries. Like all Lancashire 'cotton towns', it specialised in a particular kind of product, using Egyptian cotton (in contrast with the American that was used elsewhere) to produce high-quality yarn, which was used in the manufacture of coloured cloths for the European and American markets. Some of this weaving was done in Bolton, although more of it took place some distance away, in the specialised centres of Nelson and Colne.[3] It is therefore not surprising that Bertha's father should have begun his career as a 'half-timer', working as a 'little piecer' for a boy's wage in a spinning mill; but it is impressive that he was able to work his way up from these beginnings to a powerful position in mill management on the small and specialised weaving side of the local cotton industry, with a role in textile design and a side-line in inventing safety machinery. This brought him to the fringes of Bolton's ruling elite in the early twentieth century: being able to hire a car and driver for a holiday in Llandudno in 1914 showed impressive command over resources, at a time when cars were unusual and exciting.

Being able to pay for Bertha's post-school secretarial education in shorthand and typing, even in a small local commercial 'college', was also a measure of success. Miss Rothwell's establishment is exactly the sort of private educational enterprise that does not leave records for the historian, and we depend on reminiscences like Bertha's, or those of the poet Roy Fuller on his Blackpool school-ing at about the same time, for windows on such worlds.[4] However strong her mother's desire to stay close to her roots may have been, it seems unlikely that going into the mill, even as a weaver, would really have been a conceivable alternative for someone from such a comfortable background. Women's jobs on the spinning side, especially in the card room where the cotton was prepared for spinning, tended to be dirty, dusty, 'rough', unhealthy and badly paid by comparison.[5]

Just as overlookers in Preston's weaving sheds were able to find work in the mill for their daughters and other relatives,[6] so Bertha's father found her a place as a switchboard attendant (a classic example of the new 'white blouse' office jobs for women that emerged at the turn of the century) in the head office of his firm. She began work, in 1921, just as the post-war boom in the cotton industry was coming to an end; and when she moved to Tillotson's the printers in the following year, her wage of 30 shillings (£1.50) per week was significantly better than that of a male 'little piecer', the subordinate juvenile job on a spinning mule that her father had done, at the same age, and much more than that of an adult female card room worker, who would do very well to receive £1.[7]

As she moved out of the cotton industry into printing and then advertising, which was later (working alongside Fred) combined with small-scale manufacturing, she also placed herself at one or two removes from the troubles of the cotton industry as they accumulated during the 1920s. At the time of her marriage in 1927, Bolton's cotton trade was suffering less from trade depression and foreign competition than most of its neighbours, as the higher end of the market held up better than (for example) the coarse yarns and cloths, mainly for the Indian market, in which Blackburn and Oldham specialised.

But Bolton was already beginning to lose ground in the mid-1920s, and by 1935 its cotton output had declined by up to 40 per cent from the post-war peak year of 1924.[8] It was in 1935 that the bottom eventually fell out of both the advertising and the detergent business, and Fred's firm had to go into liquidation: an illustration of how a cumulative decline in employment and spending power in manufacturing industries could work through a local economy to damage services and hit the sale of goods whose purchase was a matter of choice rather than necessity. Fortunately, we shall see that this did not affect seaside holidays, which were already too deeply engrained in Lancashire popular culture to be lightly set aside. Bolton's population was falling slightly throughout the inter-war years, as migration to other places outweighed a small surplus of births over deaths; and it seems likely that most migrants were drawn from those with movable resources and access to capital, rather than those who were tied to the cotton industry by skills, relationships and hopes that were specific to the locality.[9] Many of Bolton's leading industrialists sold up during the inter-war years, the most prescient doing so in the speculative industrial boom of 1918–20, and headed for comfortable retirement in Blackpool, Southport or the Lake District; and they were joined by a steady stream of others, who took what they could and left the town to be run by shopkeepers and solicitors, while the remaining cotton employers diversified their interests into advertising and entertainment.[10] This seems to fit in very well with Fred's experience: he was well connected with the members of the local elite who lived in the big houses along Chorley New Road, but his own commercial leanings were towards advertising and illustration, and his parents were already resident in Blackpool and able to give Fred and Bertha a helping hand when it was needed. The time has come, indeed, to follow Fred and Bertha from Bolton to Blackpool, a path that so many others trod in these years as something more than holidaymakers.

Blackpool

In contrast with Bolton, Blackpool prospered during the 1920s and 1930s, while many of the areas from which its (by this time) traditional visitors were drawn were suffering from industrial depression and high, sometimes stratospheric rates of unemployment. It helped that Blackpool had already become a national as well as a regional resort, and that falling prices meant that those in work could still afford a holiday, even as struggling employers cut their wage-rates.[11] Even in the hard-hit weaving district around Blackburn, stories were told of people having their Blackpool holiday but returning part-way through it to draw their dole, and William Woodruff describes his mother funding a holiday by working in a brothel during the visit.[12] The former claim sounds like an 'urban legend', and the latter story was (to say the least) unusual, but hard times did not diminish the lure of Blackpool.

A survey of conditions in Lancashire reported in 1936 that the coastal area, with Blackpool at its core, 'can almost be compared with the newer industrial areas of the South' for prosperity and growth. Blackpool itself suffered from high levels of seasonal unemployment, reaching a quarter of the insured workforce in the winter of 1938; but it continued to attract migrants in very large numbers.[13] Some followed the path immortalised by Gracie Fields in the 1934 film *Sing as we go*, which used Bolton for some location filming, as she fled unemployment at home to find a summer's work in the holiday industry. Many such people became year-round residents.[14] Others, like Harold Palmer's family, were refugees from business failure, in this case in the Staffordshire Potteries, who aimed to set up in business. Palmer's parents struggled to make ends meet in a 'sunshine semi' that they could not afford, until they eventually moved up into a house that was close enough to the main holiday area to enable them to take in visitors, which is what tilted the balance towards survival and success. Many families gave up before this point.[15] But Blackpool's main goal, alongside the continuing development of its already unique holiday season (with around seven million visitors per annum in the 1930s), was to find prosperous occupants (commuters, comfortable retired residents, new and dynamic local business people) for the large numbers of semi-detached and detached houses that were spreading across the fields on the outskirts of the town, especially around the new planned leisure spaces of Stanley Park and at South Shore, reaching out to touch hands with the secure respectability of St Anne's and Lytham. Fred and Bertha's choice of residence, Ivy House, was too eccentric to fit this pattern (although it was on the fringes of the southern tip of Blackpool); but, despite their initial cash-flow problems, they were certainly desirable residents of this new and burgeoning residential Blackpool.[16]

Such developments helped to make Blackpool into one of the most dynamic and expansive seaside resorts in the world during the 1920s and 1930s. The British seaside was generally prosperous and buoyant in these years. There was no British census in 1941, due to the war, and that of 1921 was taken at the beginning of the holiday season; but between 1911 and 1951 the population of 116 seaside resorts in England and Wales grew from 1.6 million (the count was taken in April) to nearly 2.5 million. By 1951 more than one in twenty of the population of England and Wales lived in seaside resorts. In this lively company Blackpool's own growth was outstanding: by 1931 it already had over 100,000 residents, and by 1951 it had almost reached 150,000, after which it was to stagnate, not least because there was no room for further growth within its boundaries. Between 1911 and 1951 only Southend added more new inhabitants to the local total, and only Morecambe and Redcar among the top forty resorts of 1911 grew faster in percentage terms, from much lower starting figures. During this period of explosive growth Blackpool overtook Bournemouth and almost caught up with Brighton.[17]

So Fred and Bertha were moving from a town experiencing industrial decline to a setting in which growth was rapid and optimism generally high. Opportunities beckoned for the enterprising. Contemporary descriptions of the crowd at play communicate the sheer energy and joy of living that were associated with Blackpool holidays in the 1930s. Here is Charles Graves, gossip columnist and brother of the poet Robert, in 1930:[18]

Yes, Blackpool is flabbergasting. You are like a cheerful straw in an organised whirlpool of ridiculously inexpensive gaiety. Blackpool takes off its jacket to give you a good time, and give it it does. It has been described as a pleasure factory. But what a factory! It has even built its own cliffs and its own rocks. You can measure its dance floors by the acre and its bars by the furlong ... Blackpool is overpowering. Its air is so strong, its places of amusement so gigantic, its enjoyment of life so terrific, its colours so bright, that you grope for phrases to describe it adequately ... Looking out over the Mediterranean-blue sea, with the golden sands and the broad promenades, it is difficult to remember coherently how your yesterdays were spent. There lingers in the mind the memory of gigantic, gilded ball-rooms, enormous carpeted corridors, vast cafés, jazz bands, thousands of bare-headed mill girls in short printed frocks, thousands of young men in flannel trousers or plus fours, rapt audiences, multicoloured clowns, jugglers, ballet girls, Indian conjurers, Italian orchestras, automatic machines by the hundred, staggeringly long piers, the best ice-cream in the world ...

All this enthusiasm comes from someone who spent most of his time at Biarritz, Cannes, Deauville or the Lido at Venice. It was echoed by others later in the decade, such as William Holt, the eccentric Communist local councillor from Todmorden who wrote about Blackpool for Manchester's *Daily Dispatch* in August 1934, or the Mass-Observation team of 'anthropologists' who began in 1936 with the aim of studying the working class of Bolton as if they were South Sea islanders, followed their quarry to Blackpool at the annual town holidays, and wrote at length and with amazement about what they found. They were less eulogistic than Graves: Holt admitted that the sea was brown rather than blue and the Mass-Observers' fascination extended to the seamy and disreputable side of Blackpool life, especially on the Golden Mile.[19]

This, with all its problems out of season and under the surface, was the exciting Blackpool to which Fred and Bertha moved in 1935. It was not just pleasure palaces and 'mass entertainment': Blackpool was eagerly extending its attractions during the inter-war years in response to the new cults of the sun, the outdoors, health and exercise that were transforming and liberating the British seaside at this time.[20] In this spirit the local authority spent huge sums on promenade extensions and gardens, swimming pools and solaria, and the jewel in the Corporation's gleaming crown, Stanley Park.[21] Private enterprise joined in: although new boarding-houses and hotels were still being built in this period, the accommodation industry (and it *was* an industry, with more than 5000 landladies returned in the 1921 census) was also offering the fresh air and fun of the camp site and holiday camp. Seventeen of the 30 fastest-growing British resorts over this period, Blackpool included, offered holiday camp accommodation alongside the conventional landlady, as part of the development of a free, relaxed holiday atmosphere, an informality and openness that sought to emulate the perceived virtues of the Continent and distance the British seaside from Victorian stuffiness.[22]

Ivy House, as Fred and Bertha developed it, fitted perfectly into this picture. It is interesting that they did not originally envisage a holiday camp, but were thinking of running a boarding-house, despite their limited number of potential letting bedrooms, and their position on the outskirts of the town. This was a highly competitive business with tight margins, and although they had better family support and much better business skills than the Palmers, it is easy to imagine them struggling to establish the necessary 'connection' of returning visitors.[23] Running a smallholding on the fertile soil of Marton Moss also seemed a possibility until their lack of expertise and the uncertainty of their markets quickly became apparent. They did very well to be able to rent, and within a couple of years to purchase, three acres of such good agricultural and potential building land at an affordable price, and here again the ability of Fred's family to provide support (including the part played by his brother and sister-in-law in getting the camp going) was clearly crucial, along with the property Fred and Bertha already owned in Bolton. This was an unusual level of financial backing for people in their situation. They made the most of it; but it is interesting that the holiday camp development was not originally envisaged, though far from accidental: Fred had the ability to recognise the opportunity presented by the boys who arrived out of the blue with their tents, and the awareness to extend this market into something more lucrative by providing something new. Fred and Bertha earned their success.

We do not usually associate Blackpool with holiday camps, but from the 1930s onwards it acquired its share, in keeping with the free and easy holiday culture it propagated during that decade. There was already a substantial holiday camp among the sand dunes at Squire's Gate, on the borough boundary, before Fred and

Bertha developed Ivy House. This was the site of the future Pontin's camp. William Holt wrote about it in 1934, providing lyrical descriptions of sunburnt campers in all the radiance of healthy youth, while at the same time alluding to the camp's reputation for free and easy sexuality and pointing to the sensual outlines of two black cats, male and female, that adorned the gates.[24] Ivy House seems not to have gone along this route. The full-page advertisement for the Squire's Gate holiday camp in the *British Railways Holiday Guide* for 1952 featured bathing beauties and dancing, but also, more prosaically, bowls.[25] By 1939 the Sunnyhurst camp, off Highfield Road, had a half-page advertisement in the *United Kingdom Holiday Guide*, claiming to be 'Blackpool's finest holiday camp', with free parking, no extras, and an illustrated brochure for interested enquirers.[26] Ivy House, a small camp even at its peak with room for only 125 guests, apparently did not need to advertise in this way, making do with small press advertisements and word of mouth. In the late 1950s it featured in the 'Camping' section of the Ward Lock guide to Blackpool, when its chalet accommodation was listed alongside the tents at what was now Green's Holiday Camp, Squire's Gate, the 'private' caravans at Newholme, Preston New Road, and at Sunnyhurst, and the chalets and caravans at Saynor's, Preston New Road, all on what were still the semi-rural outskirts of the town.[27]

Bertha provides us with a fascinating account of the development and day-to-day running of Ivy House, which is a really important contribution to our understanding of this type of holiday camp (if indeed Ivy House can be defined as a 'type') and of neglected aspects of the history of Blackpool. It is interesting to note that her own holiday choices, although associated with the inter-war cult of fresh air and the outdoors, leant more towards the countryside and the appreciation of scenic beauty than to the crowds and commercial entertainment of Blackpool. Her descriptions of early week-end walks on the moors above Bolton remind us of the struggles to protect access to open land in this area during the late nineteenth century, and the popular traditions of rambling and hiking that are associated with the Bolton and Manchester areas.[28] Later holidays spent at Whitby, or camping at a farmhouse in the Wye Valley, or in a fisherman's cottage at St Ives, suggest an attraction to the picturesque untidiness of old 'fishing quarters' and an identification with the old, the rustic and the traditional which might be thought to sit uneasily alongside the Ivy House venture, although the house itself was perfectly compatible with these preferences.[29] Fred's enthusiasm for landscape painting, which became a shared inter-est, suggests similar values, and it is significant that part of the entertainment 'package' that Ivy House evolved included a day in the Lake District, and that holidays there with the children were followed by the establishment of a branch of the family in Bowness, while the development of a subsidiary business in Ilkley can also be fitted into this pattern.

But Blackpool was where you went to make money, and these values did not inhibit Fred and Bertha from making full use of the town's unique popular entertainment industry for the enjoyment of their visitors (and themselves), while Fred was quick to find a niche among the local entertainment entrepreneurs, politicians and even council officials. He was, in fact, a 'character' in a tradition that Blackpool treasures, a cheerful prankster and innovator who always had to have the latest gadget and flash car, would try anything once (as indicated by the early attempt to use Bob the recalcitrant horse for the abortive 'Riding Stables'), and was adept at organising and supplying entertainment for visitors who returned year after year.[30] The visit to Billy Butlin's pioneer large-scale commercial holiday camp in its first year of operation, a piece of early industrial espion-age, showed initiative, enterprise and willingness both to learn and to adapt.[31] But Ivy House was a much smaller establishment, and what stands out is the 'do-it-yourself' approach to so much of the building work and amenity provision, including the two swimming pools, coupled as it was with a recognition of the limitations of the local team when outside expertise had to be sought. Fred's ability to get on with Mr Priestley, the sanitary inspector and later the wartime billeting officer, was vital to the success of the enterprise, which could easily have been closed down at the beginning if a more literal-minded approach to regulations had been adopted; and his direct approach to the Mayor in pursuit of the relevant permissions was also characteristic. All this fitted perfectly into Blackpool traditions of how things were done, through personal lobbying and getting round the official rules; and it helped that the Corporation was not actually dominated by landladies, but by shopkeepers and professionals with a leavening of entertainment company representatives, who were happy to welcome anything that brought additional trade to the town as a whole.[32] Fred's own entertainment skills were important to the building up of the unique package that Ivy House came to offer, a mix of do-it-yourself participatory entertainment and the lavish commercial offerings at the Winter Gardens Opera House and the Palace. By this route Fred built up the contacts with the entertainment industry that led to his association with the Miss Blackpool beauty contests, and with well-known actors and singers like Violet Carson, Kathy Kirby and Mary Hopkin. Meanwhile, the post-war switch to self-catering in chalets on the 'shoulder' season, and the opportunistic development of a petrol station in response to road widening, showed a continuing thirst for innovation and profit that faded away only gradually in succeeding years. But this part of the story is best left to Bertha herself.

This is, in many ways, a classic Blackpool story as the town likes to see itself: a tale of enterprise and innovation, a modest but real success story based on recognising people's wants and preferences, and catering for them with vigour, enthusiasm and a populist sense of fun. It is a story of family enterprise, incorporating three generations of an extended family into the development of the business.

I have tried to show how it fits in with the wider trends of the time, in Bolton, Blackpool and beyond. Fred Wood was 'larger than life' in a way that conjures up the stories about other holiday camp entrepreneurs such as Billy Butlin or Fred Pontin, although he never quite managed to match their empire building abilities. But ultimately this is also a unique story, and we are privileged to have it presented to us with such lucidity, vividness and good humour by the participant herself. Read on, and enjoy.

John K Walton
Professor of Social History
University of Central Lancashire

CHAPTER 1

The Bolton years

An Edwardian childhood

One of my first memories is of walking down Blackburn Road, Bolton on Sunday afternoons, after paying a call, as a family, to my Grandma Whittle's home. My father, Joe Whittle, walked very proudly, always with his hands clasped behind his back, while my mother, Ada, my two brothers, Bert and Tom, and I, walked decorously behind.

My father was the oldest of a family of nineteen children, nine of whom died in childhood. His father died in his fifties, leaving my father virtual head of the family. To help his mother, who worked as a weaver throughout her pregnancies and widowhood, my father started work, aged about ten, as a 'half-timer' in the mill. This involved working half a day as a 'little piecer', starting at 6 am, and the other half day at school. The job of a little piecer was to piece together the broken threads in a loom. At home, my Aunt Annie, the oldest girl, looked after the younger children.

My Grandma Whittle, mother of nineteen children.

My parents Joe and Ada.

My father later progressed to become a 'tackler' (an apprentice 'loom overlooker' responsible for mending looms when they went wrong) and eventually became a fully trained loom overlooker himself.

During these years he met and married (in May 1896) Ada Crook, set up home in a small house in Latham Street on the outskirts of Bolton and started his own family, whilst continuing to help his mother with the expenses and worry of bringing up her large family. By the time I was born in June 1905, he had been promoted to the position of Inside Manager at Cobden Mill. This job entitled him to the use of a very nice semi-detached house on the main road but, unfortunately, my mother did not want to move as 'she would lose all her friends'. I always cast envious eyes at 'our' house as I went past on my way to church. It looked so wonderful to me, standing well off the road with a lovely garden and of a most unusual design; so different from the ordinary terraced houses in the area.

Our home in Latham Street was a very comfortable three-bedroom terraced house. The lower floor comprised a small front parlour and a large living room with the usual Lancashire black-leaded grate, containing a large oven on one side of a very deep fire place and a tank for water on the other. The living room was where we spent most of our time. It was always beautifully warm. Behind was quite a large kitchen, complete with a wash boiler and mangle.

My father spent some evenings designing the woven patterns for the well-known 'Osman Towels' which were made at Cobden Mill. He used to bring home squared paper and by blocking out some squares and leaving the others clear, created the patterns which were transferred to the warp in the looms. This squared paper fascinated me and I begged sheets to use and spent many enjoyable evenings at the table with him, creating my own designs.

My older brother Bert. *Myself with a family pet.*

Our family photograph, with myself (centre) and brothers Bert (right) and Tom (left).

At other times he cleared a corner in the living room to make his own invention – shaft guards. These were circular drums of pliable thick card with wooden ends, in two halves, designed to be placed over the dangerous protruding shafts which drove the automatic looms. Fast-moving shaft ends had often been the cause of very serious accidents, catching and holding clothing and long hair. The

Uncle Moses in the garden at Latham Street.

A family of inventors

Inventing seems to have run in the family. Joe Whittle's younger brother, Moses, was an engineer, inventing several safety items for bicycles; and Moses' son (Bertha's cousin) was Frank Whittle, the inventor of the jet engine. Frank was born two years after Bertha in 1907. He grew up in Coventry before moving when he was nine to Leamington Spa where Moses had bought a small engine factory.[33] As the two families lived a distance apart, Bertha did not get know Frank very well but she does recall visits when they were children.

Frank Whittle joined the RAF as a boy apprentice at Cranwell in 1923, aged sixteen. Two years later he became an officer cadet and began his study aircraft design.

shaft guard covered the whole of the moving mechanism, so rendering it safe.

My mother was a real homemaker and a marvellous cook. She was also a self-taught dressmaker and made most of our clothes, teaching me at the same time.

From the age of five I attended the local Council School. It had mixed classes but strictly segregated playgrounds, clearly marked 'Boys' and 'Girls'; and heaven help anyone caught in the wrong one. We were taught very basic but useful subjects, including housewifery for the girls and elementary wood carving and joinery for the boys. For housewifery the school provided a small terraced house where each class of girls took it in turns to keep it spotlessly clean, doing all the necessary chores including cooking dinner for the teachers, washing up and washing articles brought in by the teachers. For sport we did 'physical jerks' in the playgrounds or walked to the nearest park to play rounders.

Until we were in our teens my brothers and I spent most of our leisure time in Sunday School. We discovered poetry and adventure stories and enjoyed dances and concerts, given chiefly by ourselves; my speciality was a dialect recitation called 'Owd Boans an 'is Goose'. This was a regular request. I was also 'Fairy Flora' in the year-end pantomime. There were weekly meetings of the 'Band of Hope' teaching us the evils of drink. We were asked to 'sign the pledge' not to partake of alcohol. I must confess that most of us signed this every week, for which we received a small gift!

As we grew older about twelve of us went rambling every Saturday over the moors north of Bolton. We discovered a farm on top of Burnt Edge where the farmer's wife used to welcome us with a drink to have with our sandwiches. We subsequently spent many happy weekends there.

For one week in the summer all the mills in Bolton, together with the schools and most of the shops,

Uncle Albert, killed during the First World War.

closed down for the holidays. Many of the work people, after saving up all year, drew out their savings and flocked by train, mainly to Blackpool. Some of the more adventurous travelled as far as Morecambe. In June 1914, when we were getting past the stage of 'bucket and spade' holidays, my father hired a car, complete with driver, to take the family to Llandudno. I remember the feeling, as we drove off, of what I can only call superiority when everyone else we knew would be travelling in a crowded train.

Very soon, however, our happy, carefree life was shattered by the outbreak of the First World War and there followed four years of sadness and depression. My Uncle Albert was killed in France and my older brother Bert was called up to join the Flying Corps as a PT instructor. At home, food shortages led to rationing. I remember having to queue for hours for bacon and meat.

First steps into work

By the end of the war I was approaching the age for leaving school which raised the problem of what work I should do. I understand that two of my teachers called to see my parents to ask them 'not to put me in the mill'. Eventually my father found a 'Commercial College' nearby and enrolled me as a student.

The College was just one of a pair of semi-detached

houses on the main road. It was run by one fully
qualified teacher, Miss Rothwell, who, as well as
teaching about six pupils in the 'front room', was able
to care for her ageing mother in the same house. She
was a diligent teacher of Pitman's shorthand, typing,
instruction in business practices and elementary book-keeping. I
took the official Commercial Examination and became a fully
qualified secretary.

By this time, my father had been promoted to General Manager
of Cobden Mill and wished us to move to a more suitable place
to live. My mother, however, was still reluctant. The first I knew
was that my father came home one day and stated that we were
moving to a house in Smithills, as soon as it was built. He had
gone to an architect in Bolton and inspected plans of properties
available in the district. Our new home was to be a semi-detached
house being built next to Smithills Hall on Church Road. My
mother used to stare wistfully out of the window but gradually
came to love the new house.

I was now sixteen. At first, my father got me a job in his firm's

Cobden Mill

Cobden Mill was built in two phases at the end of the nineteenth century. The extensive site was centred on a five-storey
spinning block, with a lower warehouse and preparation block
to the side. Of flat-roof construction in brick, with a cast-iron,
concrete and steel internal structure, it is considered today a
good example of the 'moderism' of mill design. It is now a
Grade II listed building.[34]

Bertha's brothers also worked at Cobden Mill; Bert
eventually becoming Inside Manager, while Tom, although
trained as a cabinet maker, worked as a joiner.

head office at Albert Mill as a switchboard attendant. This gave me some idea of general office work and the confidence to take part in office routine. The job however was rather dreary. I looked forward to week-ends roaming over the moors, staying at the Burnt Edge farm, attending football matches at Burnden Park with my father and Saturday night dances and impromptu plays with my friends.

Soon I decided to look for a job where I could make use of my qualifications. In my spare time I visited every office I could find in Bolton town centre including Tillotson and Son Ltd, the printing and publishing firm and proprietors of the *Bolton Evening News*. Here, I enquired with trepidation of the young man who attended to me "Do you need any typists?" To my surprise, instead of fobbing me off, he said "I'll get Miss Clarkson". After asking to see my credentials and taking my name and address she said "We'll let you know". I returned to the switchboard rather discouraged and frustrated.

However, a few weeks later I received a letter from Tillotson's inviting me for an interview with Miss Clarkson. Although a very strict looking person, she was very considerate. She took me into a private room, tested my speed in shorthand and typing, asked general questions to get to know what kind of person I was, and then said, "When can you start?" The wage was around 30 shillings per week.

I started at Tillotson's as a fully blown shorthand typist; at seventeen, the youngest typist they had ever had. Each typist was dedicated to dealing with the correspondence of one man. My boss turned out to be the son of the Managing Director, Mr Shepherd, and not the most hardworking man on earth! What he did all day I don't know. What he didn't do was dictate to me on time the answers to the enquiries in the day's post until so late in the morning that it was impossible for me to have the letters of reply typed until all the other typists had finished. I was afraid I would be thought incompetent.

After some time I decided to take matters into my own hands. I simply took letters concerning various printing jobs into the works, found the foreman and asked how I could get answers to the queries. Recovering from his original surprise, he gave me all the particulars I needed and wished me luck! This became a regular routine; Mr Shepherd got away with doing the minimum of work, but I finished my job as soon as the rest of the staff which suited me very well.

I really enjoyed my excursions into the works. The men got used to seeing me around and were always ready to help, and I picked up a good working knowledge of typesetting and printing. Whilst on one of my excursions I met a Mr Greenhalgh who was very curious about my activities. When I explained he asked if I would take dictation from him, as he had no typist. Having agreed to this, I settled down now to my self-revised routine and was actually commended by Miss Clarkson for efficiency! I don't think she had any idea of what I had taken on, but I was quite happy.

This state of affairs continued for quite some time until Mr Greenhalgh told me he was leaving to form his own advertising agency. He asked if I would consider joining him as his secretary with an increased salary. I thought it would probably be a more interesting job, and accepted.

The G W Advertising Service

The agency, The G W Advertising Service, took its initials from the surnames of Mr Greenhalgh and his business partner Mr Wood. Their 'office' was a bit of a surprise. It comprised two rooms over a tailor's shop in Bradshawgate and was entered from a narrow alley with a door facing the back premises of a confectioner's shop. Through the door, up a flight of rickety stairs and there was 'the office'.

I worked mostly with Mr Greenhalgh who attended to the business side while Mr Wood did all the drawings to illustrate the adverts. We were kept quite busy, both men interviewing their own clients and meeting possible new advertisers. We introduced on to the market quite a number of new products and planned advertising programmes for local shops and businesses, placing adverts in newspapers and periodicals for which we received a 10 per cent commission.

We worked well together and with increasing success until Mr Greenhalgh's uncle died, leaving his two nephews large sums of money. It was proposed that one of the nephews, Jack Greenhalgh, would invest some of his cash in the business and be given a job. Doubtfully Mr Wood agreed. Cash was always acceptable but in no time at all it was plain that Jack could not, or would not, learn the rudiments of the business, but still insisted on having a say in the running of the firm. Mr Wood objected and justifiably decided to quit.

F Wood & Co. Advertising Service

Fred Wood now set up his own advertising agency. He had taken a postal course on the subject and was now qualified, more professionally than Mr Greenhalgh; plus he had his own talent as an acknowledged commercial artist. When he asked me to join him I was delighted. We had a good business relationship and the thought of working together where I myself would contribute to the success of the venture was exciting. Besides, I wanted to be with him.

A number of Fred's clients said they would like him to continue to handle their accounts. He also had a certain amount of commercial art in hand, so we had the nucleus of a business. We found and rented a large area over several shops in the centre of Bolton. It comprised one very large room overlooking the main road, and several small rooms to the rear which could be used as offices; one for my secretarial work, one for Fred's art work and a small storage room.

We also acquired two helpers: Eric Stanley, an ex-art pupil of Fred's; and Jack Chamberlain who had just left school and was willing to try anything. Eric was tall, fair and very handsome and charming; Jack, fairly small, sturdy, down to earth and implacable. But they became firm friends, excellent workmates and a combined asset to our business.

We were soon up and running with our new publicity idea – large, hand-painted posters, for pasting up on hoardings, made up of four separate quarters assembled together to show a complete illustration. Armed with informative sample sketches Fred concentrated on promoting to clients what we considered to be a unique method of bringing their goods and services to the notice of potential buyers. Firm orders followed from local shopkeepers and businessmen, including full-size portraits of politicians during election times.

Space on the hoardings had to be booked and paid for in advance and someone was needed with a ladder and adhesive paste. For this we employed, part time, an Irish odd-job man. He was fine, but we were to learn not to pay him a weekly wage or we would never see him again until he had drunk his way through the lot!

We also invested in a Multigraph, a new type of American duplicating machine, which printed facsimile typewritten letters which we could use as part of advertising schemes. I operated this machine, first setting up the type in separate digits in the grooves of a heavy metal drum. This was then attached to the machine and rotated by hand to print the inked type on to quarto sheets of letter headed paper.

At around this time neon signs were becoming popular for shop and hotel names and for special advertising features. Fred approached a neon manufacturer who agreed to make signs to Fred's designs and we sent Eric and Jack on an electrical training course to learn how to erect them. This created a very lucrative addition to the business.

One request came from two young men to work out a scheme for marketing a new washing tablet. They told us that this contained a very rare ingredient, making it unusually effective. We were given proof of this ambitious claim and agreed to take on the task. However, during the preliminary planning of the advertising campaign the two men fell out with one another. One decided to market the product on his own; the other offered to sell to us his rights in the recipe, as he had other plans. We thought this could be a good sideline and took up his offer.

'Wash with Wish'

Manufacturing the washing tablet ourselves meant a complete change of work for us. It required machinery for mixing the ingredients to the right consistency to make 3 inch square semi-solid tablets, and space for the handling and shaping the tablets and then packing them neatly into printed instruction leaflets, with outer wrappers containing the name. We rented a dilapidated three-storey warehouse and used a small, second-hand concrete mixer for the actual mixing. A long trestle table for shaping and packing the tablets, a few upright chairs and we had our workshop. Fred designed the wrapper and after much thought we decided to call it 'Wish' and use the slogan 'Wash with Wish'.

To make up the work force we were joined by Fred's younger brother, Billie; Eric and Jack; and a friend of mine from church. Sitting round the table packing the tablets proved a great opportunity for entertaining discussions. I remember one very heated argument about spiritual matters, which ended with Eric, who was 'agin' everything, throwing up his arms and declaring "To Hell with Religion!" He did this with such force that the back legs of his chair went right through the floor, with him going helplessly backwards. I don't think I have ever seen such genuine terror on anyone's face. He obviously thought 'the Almighty' was taking his revenge.

Fred was again the salesman, visiting all the Co-ops and corner shops in the area and creating a reasonable demand. Later we advertised for representatives to create a demand in Yorkshire and Westmorland as well as Lancashire. In the printed instructions on the wrapper we offered a scheme whereby customers could save the wrappers, return them, and gain prizes including cut glass bon-bon dishes, vases and wine glasses.

Eventually, we gave up the labour-intensive advertising posters and moved our office to a more desirable location on St George's Road. The new place had two ground-floor rooms which served as an office and studio and a number of bed-sits above. As the bed-sits were already let, this provided a little more steady income.

Engaged to Fred

As the business developed, Fred and I became more emotionally involved. His interests, however, apart from the business, were very different from mine. For a start he was six years older than I. His 'set' was the rather 'fast' type, pairing off from their early teens. In Bolton the girls were known as the 'Bolton Beauties' and the boys the 'Smart' set. Long before I knew him, he and his older brother Jack were 'escorting' twin sisters, and when I first met him he was engaged to a very pretty blonde, one of the 'Chorley New Road' set. However, when Fred found that his fiancée was interested in another man he quickly and, I think gladly, broke off the engagement.

Returning from holiday in Whitby with friends, I was greeted with open arms and "I've missed you".

Fred and his older brother Jack.

Jack was an early fighter pilot and flew a Sopwith Pup. He was killed in action in the First World War.

Fred joined the army towards the end of the war as a PT instructor. That's him, seated centre, with a cigarette in mouth.

From then on it was plain sailing towards an engagement. Fred formally asked and received my father's permission but my mother was 'not amused' and continued to call him 'Mr Wood'.

I remember a very enjoyable holiday during our engagement, staying in the Wye Valley at a farm at Hope-under-Dinmore. Fred slept in a small bivouac tent in the orchard and I slept in a crooked room in the ancient farmhouse. We dined in the huge kitchen with the farmer, his wife and family and all of the farm hands.

On our return from Hope we started to make plans towards when we would be married. First we looked for a home. There were lots of the usual terraced houses available, but we wanted something near the outskirts of Bolton, ideally in one of the suburbs where new houses were being built. Having seen proposals for four new two-bedroom bungalows in Ox Hey Lane, Horwich, we decided that one of these could be just what we wanted. We learned the completion date and made this the date of our wedding.

My father offered to put down the deposit as a wedding present so we were able to have some extras included in the building and to furnish it better than we had expected. For instance, we arranged for the dining room to be lined with oak panelling to match a specially hand-made oak refectory table. We also managed to find a period sideboard, known as a Butler's Server, six rush-seated ladder-backed chairs and a genuine Windsor chair. The sitting room we kept quite simple, including two brocade covered chairs and a piano. Fred's father said he would buy us a bed – just as well as we were running out of cash!

Early married life

We were married in June 1927 when I was twenty-one. I had my twenty-second birthday during our honeymoon, and never even realised it!

For our honeymoon, my father lent us his Belsize Bradshaw sports car. We travelled south, calling first at the farm at Hope-under-Dinmore, then in easy stages to Devon and Cornwall, where we finally stayed for a week in a fisherman's cottage in St Ives.

Our first child, Corrine, was born in October 1928. I continued to work full time, spending some hours at home and some at the office. To avoid taking Corrine into the atmosphere of the busy

Our wedding day.

town, we hired a French girl, Denise, to baby-sit during the day. In January 1931, our second child, Keith, was born. By now, Denise had gone back home, but with the help of neighbours across the road, I managed to cope with the two children and the secretarial work Fred brought home.

When the time came to find a school for Corrine, we discovered there was literally no school for miles. Very reluctantly we decided to move to where there was a choice. We found a large semi-detached house to let, next to the park on Chorley New Road, within walking distance of Bolton town centre and the schools. It had ample room for me to have a proper office, as well as three good-sized bedrooms. We let the bungalow and so had the cash available for the house.

Our furniture, which had been perfect for the bungalow, looked ridiculous in these more palatial rooms, but we settled in comfortably enough. Fred drove Corrine to school in the morning on his way to work and I walked with Keith in the push-chair, through the park, to pick her up in the afternoons.

This worked very well. The business was still competitive and successful; I had a decent office and Corrine was happy in her school. We had a period of quiet contentment, or so we thought.

The Great Depression

In the early 1930s our business became one of the victims of what was to be called 'The Great Depression'. Clients started reluctantly to cancel their advertising agreements owing to their own loss of business. No-one could afford neon signs, and in a single month every one of our representatives for Wish failed to send in their takings. We in turn were unable to pay our suppliers. We got together with our account-ant to review our position. One thing we did not want to happen was that one of our creditors would cause us to be declared bankrupt, when we would all lose everything.

We were advised to calculate how much we could afford to pay, call a Meeting of Creditors and offer them a certain percentage of each pound we owed them. Very much to our gratification, they accepted unanimously. We made a promise that, as soon as we were able, we would settle all debts completely. We asked to retain our car, an Austin Seven saloon, as a necessity for Fred's ability to acquire new business, and also our bungalow. This they agreed to;

A family photograph in the garden at Ox Hey Lane, with our Alsatian, Laska. When I took Corrine for a walk in the pram, down the steep hill, Laska helped me, with the aid of strong rope, to pull the pram back up.

Portrait photographs of the two of us.

so, for the time being, although we had no capital and very little income, we were free from debt. A few of our clients still wanted us to continue to handle their advertising, so this was some income to cover our mortgage, but there was no new business to be had in Bolton, so we had to find some way to carry on.

CHAPTER 2

The move to Blackpool

Ivy House

Fred's parents, Fred and Helen, were retired and living in Blackpool. From visits to them we got the idea that if we could get a suitable house there to rent, we could make enough money supplying bed and breakfast to add to our small income, perhaps to get by until things got better.

We went to Blackpool for a few days, staying with Fred's parents. There were plenty of houses to let, but none with sufficient sized bedrooms for our scheme, nor within our price range. On our way home we took a different route out of the town, along Common Edge Road beside Marton Moss, and there, by the roadside, we noticed a long cottage-type building displaying a 'To Let' sign. Grasping at any possibility we stopped to examine it.

The building stood quite isolated on what appeared to be its own land. Peering through the front windows we saw what appeared to be a large kitchen, running from front to back and, on the other side of a very solid central door, a small sitting room. These rooms took up half the length of the building; the other half was a plain wall, with a single door to the front, a huge door to the rear and one very dilapidated high window. On going round the back, we found outhouses, three 60 foot greenhouses (most of the panes were broken), a substantial potting shed and about 3 acres of land. Half the land was under crops, while the other half was divided into two large grassed areas, one with five respectable looking caravans, all occupied. It had great possibilities.

We got the name of the owner from the sign and went to see him for further particulars and the key. He told us that the name of the property was Ivy House. Getting the key was one thing, but getting the heavy studded front door open was quite another. We struggled for ages but finally got it to move and entered a small hallway with doors to left and right and stairs ascending straight ahead.

The door on the right opened inwards: we pushed it and promptly fell full length down the high step inside. We were prone in the kitchen! Undeterred, we got up and proceeded with our exploration. In the stone-flagged kitchen were a large black-leaded grate (which brought back memories of my childhood home in Latham Street) and a 'slop stone' instead of a sink. Just off the kitchen was a square space leading to the back entrance. Here also were doors to the sitting room and to a spacious walk-in larder containing a huge slab obviously used for cold storage of food. The larder ran the full length of the sitting room. In the sitting room itself, the wallpaper was literally hanging off the wall. The stairs went up between the two main ground floor rooms, sloping drunkenly, leading to a small landing and corridor, off which were three decent-sized bedrooms and, to our surprise, a modern flush toilet! The corridor and rooms had sloping floors and ceilings, but were light and airy. This was clearly the house part of the building.

Entry to the other half of the building was via a huge sliding wooden door. To open it we had to put our shoulders to one end and push. Inside was a revelation! Two large, squarish empty spaces (one with two horse stalls), with a smaller space between divided by rough brick walls. The floors were also of brick. The upper rooms were supported on dark wooden beams: to one side a half-sized room reached by an upright cat ladder; to the other a full-sized room which we thought had once been a hayloft. This was clearly a barn or stable of some sort, attached to the house.

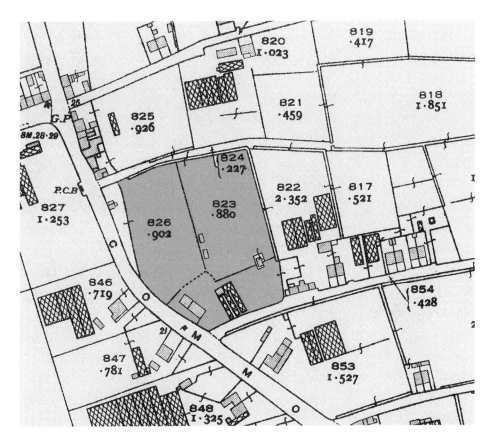

An extract from the 25" to the mile map, showing Ivy House, the greenhouses and adjacent land (reproduced from the 1938 Ordnance Survey Map).

We postponed our journey home and returned to Fred's parents, full of ideas. Ivy House was the answer to our problems, but there was no electricity, no hot water system, no bathroom and only one cold water tap. And there was one very big snag; the rent on the property was payable in advance, annually. Although the amount required was not large when broken down to a weekly rental, we still could not find one year's rent in advance unless we sold our bungalow, which was rented, and one of our prime sources of income. Our only other income was from the bed-sits and Fred's remaining clients.

If we lived at Ivy House we calculated that we could generate additional income from renting the caravans and our work premises in Bolton. This would go some way towards covering our repayments. There was also the possible return from the use of the three greenhouses when repaired, and from the arable crops, but we knew nothing about running a small holding. However, we could see that if we used our initiative, and were prepared to ask people who did know about these things, we would have the means of making a living.

After discussing the various options with Fred's parents, Fred's father generously offered to lend us the cash for the year's rent in

Vernacular buildings of Marton Moss

Whitewashed cobble and clay buildings were a common feature along the Fylde coast and edges of the mosslands, the building materials being free, plentiful and readily to hand. This type of wall construction was characteristic of the eighteenth century, although earlier examples are known. In later times, particularly on Marton Moss, the clay was used for brick-making. To judge from Bertha's description and the materials used, Ivy House would appear to have been a two-phase development; an eighteenth-century house with perhaps a nineteenth-century barn attached. The property was evidently a rundown smallholding by the time Fred and Bertha took it over. Walker's Hill Farmhouse on Midgeland Road, not dissimilar to Ivy House, is now a Grade II listed building and described as the only surviving example in the Blackpool area. A small, eighteenth-century cottage, also listed Grade II, lies close to the site of Ivy House in the area known as Blowing Sands.[35]

advance and a little extra for repairs. This was all we needed; the incoming rents would repay the loan. We stayed over to complete the transaction and returned to Bolton to start the process of uprooting ourselves, what was left of our business, letting off our properties and then saying our goodbyes. It was 1935.

A new home and business

Whilst we were busy in Bolton, we sent Eric and Jack to strip the walls and run electric wiring through the house part of the building. They discovered that the walls were about 2 feet thick and built using cobbles. We guessed it must have been at least 300 years old: the brick frontage and roof being later renovations. The cobbles made it impossible to make grooves in the walls to run the electric cable so all the wiring had to be fixed to the inside face of the walls and then covered over. Very soon the house was ready to move into.

Eric and Jack stayed on to help us to get things straight and to make the necessary alterations. We started by subdividing the large kitchen into a kitchen and breakfast room. The new kitchen had a continuous line of storage cupboards and a working surface with a window in the back wall. The breakfast room, with a circular table, had two windows; one in the front wall and one overlooking the side garden. The sitting room, we were surprised to find, was big enough to hold our refectory table, sideboard, ladder-back chairs and two small easy chairs.

Upstairs, the spacious main bedroom was over the kitchen with an alcove over the stairs. The room had a front window and another overlooking the side garden. We covered the floor with polished oak squares. However, we encountered a snag when we came to erect our beds. As we stood back to view our handiwork both beds started slowly rolling on the polished floor, finally finishing up against the wall at the other end of the room. We hadn't reckoned with the sloping floor and the casters on the beds! This was quickly rectified. For the time being, the children slept in the alcove in two small beds Fred made.

The landing at the top of the stairs, next to the existing toilet, was just big enough to take a full-size bath and wash bowl, so we had these and a hot water system installed and built a partition and door across the landing to create a bathroom.

The other two bedrooms, one of which had been occupied by Eric and Jack during the main building work, were now decorated and fitted out with reasonable looking second-hand furniture. We later knocked a doorway through the wall of the third bedroom to provide separate bedrooms for the children.

The refurbishment finished, we were now ready to put into being our original business idea of supplying bed and breakfast. We had room for up to three paying guests.

Although we were in Blackpool, and paying fairly high rates for our property, curiously Ivy House was just outside the catchment area for the nearby new school. The children therefore had to attend the small village school on Marton Moss. We were not happy with this arrangement and after taking stock of our financial position and making many enquiries, we finally found, in St Anne's, an inexpensive Catholic Prep School run by nuns. We were promised that no religious pressure would be put on the children. We found out later that the nuns' idea of no religious pressure meant leaving the children to their own devices during the many periods of Catholic instruction, and I think listening outside the classroom door, which made Corrine very curious.

Market gardening and 'Bob' the horse

As well as the income generated from paying guests, we had to find a way to make the most of the 3 acres of land behind the house. Across the road from us was a very smart new bungalow, behind which were large greenhouses and land neatly planted with rows of lettuces, cauliflowers and flowers of all description. Obviously a very well run market garden which we eyed with envy.

We were very surprised and pleased when the man from this bungalow came to ask us if he could beg some of our soil. He told us that on our side of the road the soil was black, peaty, very friable and very good growing land; on his side, however, the soil was too sandy and needed mulching to make it productive. He wanted our very rich soil to start off his seedlings, particularly the tomatoes he grew in his greenhouses.

He proved to be a fount of knowledge. We learnt about sowing seeds, transplanting seedlings, preparing greenhouse soil, stringing tomato plants and growing vegetables outdoors, especially cauli-flowers which we practically lived on one year. By this time, Fred's younger brother Billie had married and brought his bride Muriel to live with us. I don't think she had any idea what she was coming into but she was a great help.

We soon established that the field would have to be ploughed before our seedlings could be planted out. Fred made enquiries of our neighbours about a plough and finally found one which needed a lot of cleaning up and oiling but which we thought we could use. All we needed now was a horse to pull it.

We had, in a caravan parked for winter living, a gypsy who happened to need a horse because he wanted to move further south. As there was a yearly horse show in a nearby village, Fred offered to drive him there to find one. They returned in pouring rain; Fred first in the car, and much later the gypsy riding a horse.

When we asked how they got on, Fred told us that our gypsy friend hadn't found a horse suitable for long road journeys, but that he, Fred, had bought one. We were surprised, to say the least, but my father who was staying with us at the time said he wouldn't have been surprised if he had bought an elephant!

We put the horse, or 'Bob' as it came to be known, in one of the stalls, but we hadn't the slightest idea how to treat him. Again we had to rely on help from the neighbours, who responded with some amusement. They informed us about suitable food and bedding; and one thing we learned was how to get him to move to one side whilst we cleaned out the stall. Apparently, the vernacular command in Lancashire was 'ston o'r', which in plain English meant 'stand over'. Muriel was intrigued and thought she would try this out. She called 'ston o'r' and Bob did! The trouble was that he 'stood over' towards where she was standing and practically flattened her against a wall!

We had difficulty finding a suitable collar with hooks for chains to attach to the plough. When we eventually did find one, we enthusiastically tried it on Bob. We held it in the position we thought it should go and two of us pushed as hard as we could but it wouldn't go over his head. All it did was flatten his ears and go no further. Bob stood this very patiently, but after again consulting our neighbour we turned the collar round, so that the larger part went over the top of Bob's head, and then turned it round again when it was on his neck.

Now came the time to get Bob and the plough together. The collar was safely on and the plough cleaned and both ready to be connected by chains. We brought Bob out of his stall and put the plough in place behind him, attaching the chains to the collar. However, as soon as Bob felt the chains on his legs as he moved, up went his back legs taking the plough, in bits, with them! We learned later that

he was a 'trotter' and so had never experienced the feel of chains on his legs. After that we got the field ploughed professionally so we were able to plant out our vegetables.

The problem now was what to do about Bob. Fred bought a riding saddle and tried riding him along Common Edge Road, but in spite of all his pleas to "Gid-up" Bob would only move at a very slow walk. Finally, Fred decided he wasn't going to get any faster and turned Bob round for the return journey. As soon as Bob was facing home he set off at a quick trot with Fred holding on for dear life. Nevertheless, we put up a sign outside, saying 'Riding Stables', and waited for customers. But the idea was not a success, so when the gypsies arrived the following winter we were able to sell Bob at a reasonable profit.

We had arranged with a firm of haulage contractors to collect our greenhouse lettuces and deliver them early in the mornings to markets in Leeds and Bradford. The marketers paid the haulage contractor the going rate for the produce and they in turn deducted their costs and paid us, monthly, what was left. Although this meant that we had to rise very early to have our lettuces picked, hand washed and packed attractively in boxes in good time, the routine worked well until one month, instead of a cheque for the sale of the produce, we received a bill for the haulage and nothing for the lettuces.

There had been a glut of lettuces on the market, so that month there was no income. Although Fred took supplies to Bolton when he went to see his few clients, and we had a few good customers locally, it was a bleak and uncertain outlook. We decided that, taking into account our inexperience, the return was not worth the work.

Market gardening on Marton Moss
The development of Blackpool in the late nineteenth century resulted in a rapid expansion of the market gardening industry. Acres of mosslands were put under glass and mounting quantities of horticultural produce were exported to the industrial towns and cities of northern and central England. In addition to the famous 'Blackpool Tomatoes', produce included lettuces, forced mint, parsley, cucumbers, mustard, cress, cauliflowers, sweet peas, carnations and chrysanthemums.[36]

The camp site

One day there was a knock at the door. I answered it and found two small boys with heavy looking packs on their backs who asked "Can we pitch our tents on your land, Missus?" I was a bit nonplussed and they said "We came last year". Fred heard this and appeared behind me asking "How much did you pay?" The answer, "Six pence a night each". Fred, having made a quick calculation, said "Come on", and after dinner put up a sign outside saying 'Tent Site'.

Throughout that summer we had a stream of youths with tents of all shapes and sizes, and also some people with trailer caravans. We left the bottom field clear for camping and used the top field as a recreational area which was much appreciated and attracted more business. People from the camp site used to come to our back door asking if they could buy dinners. More than once I had to catch the family when they had their dinners in front of them, ready to be eaten, saying "Don't eat that, I've sold it" and whipped the dinners away. The family didn't go without (I could always make something else) but I got into the habit of making more than we needed.

An inspector calls

The camp site and dinners provided a nice supply of extra income. That was until one fateful day when we had a visit from a Mr Priestley, the sanitary inspector. After walking round the site he came to see us. His first remark was "You can't do this, you know" and then proceeded to tell us why and what we couldn't do. It appeared that although we had a licence for the five residential caravans, we had to have a further licence before we could take any more caravans or tents for holidays, without proper sanitation.

This was shattering news as we had been planning for a further season. He told us we would have to provide a proper plan for a block of toilets, bath and washing facilities, with the necessary septic tank, drainage and footpaths, and then submit this to the Planning Board of Blackpool Council. We suspected that the Council, being mostly composed of the main holiday hosts in the town, would be against anything which took possible business away from the central area; so we did not think we would have a chance of getting our plan approved.

Happily, Mr Priestley and Fred developed a mutual respect. Mr Priestley helped us with suggestions about an acceptable plan, put us in touch with workmen, and actually gave us a good reference. Unfortunately, our plan was opposed at the first planning meeting, so Fred went to see the Mayor, who happened to come from Bolton, and turned on the charm, explaining exactly our overall idea for the site. The Council members came to inspect and at the next planning meeting our plans were passed. After a few fits and starts we had the whole thing ready in time for the start of the season.

CHAPTER 3

Starting the holiday camp

Early beginnings

Now that we had a licence for camping, we gave up the bed and breakfast idea and started to grow more enterprising. When we saw an advertisement in the local paper, offering for sale army bell tents complete with wooden floors and a number of army beds and blankets, we were definitely interested. Fred went to see and bought the lot – twelve tents with four beds and blankets in each.

We erected the tents over the stout wooden floors and equipped each with a folding table and four chairs, a Primus stove and a full set of crockery, cutlery and cooking utensils bought from Woolworth's. Then we used our advertising experience to attract holiday occupants. One single column inch advert in a Sunday newspaper produced enough bookings for the middle of the season and a sign on the roadside – 'Ivy House Camp' – brought enough passing business for the rest of the season. We charged 35 shillings per week for each tent.

Although all cooking essentials were provided, we were still being asked for cooked dinners, which gave us a new idea.

We still had plenty of unoccupied land so thought we would experiment by building small huts or chalets as sleeping accommodation, with full board included. As we already had all necessary facilities installed, we had no difficult in getting planning permission. Using asbestos, we built four chalets to begin with, in a horseshoe shaped site, with two bunk beds in each.

Our plan for providing food was to turn the barn and stable area into a dining room and, if we could get a licence, a small bar. Having been granted a licence, we made a doorway through the dividing wall at the back of the larder, making a direct route between the kitchen and the proposed dining room and bar. The huge sliding door was taken down (what a job!) and a completely new entrance comprising a central door and side window created. Inside, the floor was concreted over and the internal brick walls removed to form one large room. To replace the load-bearing wall, we inserted a length of very strong tramline which we obtained from the Council. We knocked holes in the front wall to make three small windows and replaced the back window and door with new windows to match. The walls were rough plastered, the beams cleaned and the supporting tramline boxed in. Finally, the whole area was decorated and the floor covered with a hardwearing, traditional patterned carpet.

To make use of the upper floor spaces we bought an old stair-case to replace the original cat ladder. This led to what we now made into a play area with a table tennis table in the old hayloft. So we now had a recreation area available in the same building as the dining room and bar, with a direct link to our own accommodation so we were always there to keep our eyes on what was going on.

We called our new business 'Ivy House Holiday Camp' and formed a limited company comprising Fred, Billie, Muriel and myself. At the same time we bought the house and land outright. All had been achieved almost entirely by our own little group. Jack remained with us but Eric had already left. We were often dog tired but still enthusiastic after work. There were lots of scary moments, but we also had good fun, gained great satisfaction and certainly enjoyed the chance to use our own initiative.

Ivy House, with our Humber Super Snipe shooting brake parked outside.

A trip to Butlin's

It was about this time we read of a new and very popular type of holiday camp called Butlin's, similar but much larger than ours and providing a complete, inclusive programme. Fred and I were very interested and saw no reason why we could not extend our site, build more chalets and perhaps dispense with the tents. We booked a week's stay at Butlin's Skegness Holiday Camp to weigh up the possibilities.

We were very impressed with the layout at Skegness. We haunted the builders who were erecting more chalets, took note of their methods, attended the shows and competitions and came away full of certainty that we could achieve our own version which would be less frenetic and more easy going.

After reporting back to Billie and Muriel, who also liked the idea, we decided to apply for permission to build similar chalets along the edge of the bottom field, still leaving plenty of play area. We thought four blocks of four chalets would be ideal. Permission granted we went ahead with the aid of a concrete mixer, spades and trowels using the same methods we had observed at Butlin's. (Our earlier asbestos chalets were demolished.) We placed three-

Butlin's Skegness Holiday Camp

Skegness was the first of Billy Butlin's purpose-built holiday camps in Britain. Opened in April 1936, it became the blueprint for a number of similar commercial camps across the country. The Skegness camp's capacity rose from 500 to around 1200 during the first season and had increased to 2000 by the end of the year. The original chalet buildings were of timber-frame construction with asbestos panels. Advertising literature at the time was keen to emphasise that the chalets were designed like little houses, featuring 'electric light, running water, comfortable beds with interior spring mattresses' adding up to 'a luxurious home of your own.' One of the original 1936 timber chalets preserved at the site is now a Grade II listed building.[37]

quarter beds or two single beds in each chalet and I made all the frilled counterpanes and floral matching curtains. The outsides of the chalets were painted white and the roofs red.

Welcome Hall

We realised that we would need more space for feeding and entertaining the extra campers, so we began to plan a separate dining hall immediately behind the house. At the end of the season, we set about preparing the floor and constructing a skeleton of strong timber posts for each wall flat on the ground. Many hands were then needed to direct each post into its upright position and attach them to the wooden beams of the floor. The walls were lined inside with plywood panels and outside coated with a sand and cement render on an extended mesh base. We couldn't tackle the flat roof so employed specialist roofers for this. It was a very challenging and satisfactory job and we had enormous fun doing it and solving all the problems which arose constantly. When the building inspector arrived to view the shell of the hall, he said he had never known any building being constructed in this way, but he still passed it.

The finished building had windows all round, except the wall facing the house where we made a small stage. Between the hall and the house we built a connecting passage providing a direct link to the kitchen where we installed a new Aga cooker. Floral curtains, a shiny red polished floor and tables with colourful cloths made a very attractive dining room. We called it 'Welcome Hall'.

Moving the dining room freed up space in Ivy House itself. Here we extended the bar area to create what we called 'The Tudor Club'.

The exterior of Welcome Hall.

The interior of Welcome Hall set out for dining.

Further developments

Welcome Hall was a great success. Holiday makers were booking from one season to the next and increasing in number. Each winter we built more chalets until we had accommodation for 125 campers.

For outside amusements we laid a tennis court, a decent-sized

Our chalets, built in the same way as Welcome Hall, were ranged around three sides of the bottom field with a putting green in the middle.

putting green and planned a swimming pool at the far end of the top field. Even with the best will in the world we knew we couldn't manage to dig out the hole for the pool ourselves, so we engaged a man with a digging machine to do the job. The hole was the width of the top field and about half as wide and, conveniently, as the ground was sloping, we had a natural deep and shallow end for the water, about 4 foot sloping to 6 foot.

For the reinforced concrete base of the pool we scoured the area asking our neighbours if they had any old bedsteads or anything made of strong metal which we could have. We laid what we acquired in the bottom of the hole as neatly as possible and then poured a thick layer of concrete over the lot, leaving a drainage hole. Concrete steps were built into one corner and we were then ready for the walls to be added. These were constructed by pouring concrete between wooden shuttering boards set about 9 inches apart positioned all round the inside of the hole, standing about 2 feet higher than the ground outside. Against the outside face of the protruding walls we built up the soil taken from the hole, leaving a space to enter the pool. The base and inside faces were finished with a smooth coating and the whole treated with a special water-resistant paint, especially formulated for swimming pools.

We now only needed the water to swim in. The first filling was done by the local Water Board but we wanted to be able to take fresh water to top up the pool from the stream running into the dyke which ran along the edge of the top field. However, before we could use this water it had to be cleansed and chlorinated. We made enquires to a firm in the Midlands who supplied the special kind of shale needed for this purification and invested in the necessary apparatus. Unfortunately, this did not stop algae forming round the edges of the pool and it was a constant fight to keep the water clear; this despite Keith's best efforts at cleaning the edges every morning before going to school and then raking the leaves off the water in the evening.

A film career nipped in the bud

Meanwhile, Fred, who had always been a keen photographer, became involved with some people who wanted to open a film studio in Blackpool. They got together and acquired an option on a sizeable piece of land on the outskirts of the town on which to build this studio. The first film was to be *Love on the Dole* by Walter Greenwood, to be made with his full approval and starring Gracie Fields. All the arrangements had been made to form a company to be launched on the Stock Exchange. Financial matters were completed and contracts signed, so Fred went to London for the launch. It was December 1936.

He had been in London for two days when
Edward VIII abdicated. The bottom fell out of the
Stock Market; all trading ceased, so our company was
never quoted and the whole thing fell through. Fred
returned home a very disappointed man, only to be met
with the even sadder news that, whilst he was away, his mother
had died.

Love on the Dole

Walter Greenwood's book about the depression years in
Salford did not make an immediate impact when first published
in 1933: however, when it was dramatised by Ronald Gow and
shown at the Garrick Theatre, Altrincham, it became a best
seller. The play later went on the stage in London and New
York with Wendy Hiller, Ronald's wife, taking the lead.

Two attempts were made in 1936 to turn the play into a
film: the first by Gaumont British in March and the second by
Atlantic Productions in June; but both failed to pass the censor.
It is conceivable that Fred was involved in the Atlantic
Productions attempt a few months before the Abdication.
Bertha certainly recalls that he went to meet an American
director in London at about that time. Atlantic Productions
were one of a number of small film companies set up in the
1930s that went out of business during the ensuing financial
crisis.[39]

Love on the Dole was eventually made into a film in 1941
starring Deborah Kerr.

CHAPTER 4

The war years

Our plans to offer inclusive holidays were not impeded too much by the war. We were not expected to close as some other camps like Squires Gate and so were able to attract visitors during the summer months, though the camp was commandeered at times for evacuees, airmen and soldiers.

Feeding the RAF

During the early months of the war Liverpool was being bombed practically every night and so Blackpool, being the nearest airport, was where some of the fighters took off to intercept the bombers.

Some of our wartime campers. Note the reflectors on the headlamps of the motorbikes.

Digging for Victory. Our market gardening experience was revived during the war to provide food for the camp and the RAF. Agricultural work like this meant that some of our staff could avoid the call-up.

There was also hundreds of RAF 'rookies' training at the airport and sleeping in various boarding houses in the town.

At the instigation of Mr Priestley, who was now the Billeting Officer for Blackpool, Fred was sent for by the local RAF Commanding Officer and asked to arrange catering at the airport. Fred took stock of the rooms available on the airport premises and found a very large space suitable for a dining room and also one which could be used as a kitchen. He was instructed to obtain the necessary equipment and prepare the rooms for use. Billie was to be in charge of the kitchen with the help of RAF staff, although he was later drafted to work in the Vickers Aircraft Factory nearby.

We advertised locally for girls to serve the meals and, as this work would exempt them from the 'call-up' to National Service, we had quite a choice applying. I made special costumes for them – black taffeta with little white pinnies. The girls were a great success with the men and were dubbed 'Mr Wood's Young Ladies'. The numbers to feed steadily increased to 1,000 men and eventually we also catered for the Officers' Mess, the Sergeants' Mess and the Mobile Canteen serving the men working on the aircraft on the ground.

One day there was a 'phone call from the CO: "Mr Wood, get a place for officers' wives to stay, as now when there's a flap on, the pilots are sequestered all over the bloody place". So Fred made enquiries about a small hotel and eventually found Red Court. This was ideally located near the sea front, opposite the solarium, and within walking distance of the airport, was fully furnished, and could provide accommodation for about thirty wives. Fred bought it immediately. Putting in a manageress, and using part-time workers and my Aunt Kate from Bolton (one of my father's sisters) as cook, we were ready to start.

Camp commandeered

While Fred attended to matters at the airport, I was on duty at the camp. Mr Priestley had commandeered some of our chalets as accommodation for evacuees from Manchester – fifty pregnant women with their children; quite a disreputable lot! As Jack had been called up for National Service and most of our staff girls had returned home at the outbreak of the war, we had only a skeleton staff of mostly part-time middle-aged women to keep the place clean. We couldn't afford any more staff on the small allowance we received.

Unfortunately, despite drawing up a cleaning rota, the evacuees refused to do anything! I think they thought that, this being Blackpool, they were on holiday. In the evenings, quite a number of the women went up to the pub, leaving the children to run wild on the camp.

The situation was extremely hard work, particularly for Muriel

An aerial photograph of the camp, to the right of the airport and aircraft factory, taken in August 1945 (courtesy of English Heritage, NMR).

and I, as we also had a number of campers on holiday to cater for, and we both happened to be pregnant ourselves. When our doctor came to see Muriel and learned what we were attempting to do, he was concerned for our condition and got in touch with Mr Priestley. Thankfully, Mr Priestley was able to find alternative accommodation for the evacuees in several small hotels on South Shore.

In their place we were commandeered to take a unit of airmen from the airport. The unit had its own cooks, so we shared our kitchen with them; they preparing meals for the airmen while we cooked for our own campers. This worked perfectly well, apart from certain exuberances on the part of the airmen, who seemed to think that the flat roof of Welcome Hall was there for them to carry out 'high jinks' after a night out.

The airmen were with us only a short time. Soon afterwards, we were told, in great secrecy, to expect a number of soldiers and to have everything ready for instant use. When they arrived, having marched, after a fashion, from South Shore railway station, we realised we were playing host to some of the men who had survived Dunkirk. The troop had their own Sergeant, who was in as bad a shape as his men, but he still kept strict discipline. After a night's rest, the soldiers were mustered still wearing their soiled and torn uniforms. They stood to attention by the side of their chalet doors whilst the Sergeant inspected inside and then marched up to Welcome Hall where we had prepared to breakfast. This happened every morning.

While they were with us, the camp was kept well cleaned and there was no rowdyism (unlike the airmen). The soldiers simply relaxed and made the most of the facilities on offer. Although they

A court martial

Mary Chamberlain, Jack's wife, worked at the camp during the war while Jack saw active service in India. She distinctly remembers a court martial taking place in the camp bar. The culprit was one of the soldiers from Dunkirk who unceremoniously had his cap knocked off his head before he entered the room.

With Fred and Frankie down by the
chalets.

A family photograph taken outside
Welcome Hall.

didn't stay long, I must say that I have never admired any group of
men as I did these.

Our third child, a girl, was born in February 1940. We named
her Frances but she was always known as Frankie. A few weeks
earlier, Muriel had had a boy, Donald. In anticipation, Billie and
Muriel ceased living at Ivy House and moved to a small grocery
shop they rented in St Anne's.

CHAPTER 5

Life in the camp

Recruiting staff

As we required 'artistes' to perform a show and also girls to serve the meals, we decided it would be a good idea to combine these jobs and have the same girls do both. We placed a small advert in the *Stage* magazine thinking that the chance of a job for the whole summer would appeal to stage people. Initially we only had one applicant, Yvonne Miles from Wales. She sang and was prepared to help in other ways, and very soon became like one of the family living with us in the house. Further adverts in the *Stage* brought a bigger response and Fred arranged to meet a number of applicants at a small hotel in London. He chose three girls with different talents, a pleasant manner and appearance, and also a pianist with very good references. We also required kitchen staff every season. Although Muriel and I had done all the cooking before now, and had built up a good reputation, we needed help catering for 125 campers every day.

Some of the staff girls and their foibles were a great source of amusement. I distinctly remember Tina, a local girl, with her high heels and tight skirts and 'bouffant' hair do, tripping about like 'Betty Boop' of cartoon fame. To our surprise she turned out to be the 'Moll' of the local 'Mafioso', who used to drive up in an enormous car to take her out. And who could forget 'The Amazons', a trio of girls nearly 6 feet tall, who came to us straight from the army. They sang very well and with much comic feeling, 'Baby, its cold outside ...', to tremendous applause. They were great

Yvonne joins the staff

Yvonne replied to the advert in the *Stage* aged seventeen, sending a copy of her photograph. She never had an interview or audition. Remarkably, she still has Bertha's letter inviting her to join the staff, dated 20th April 1940, in which Bertha wrote:

> Although you do not play any instrument, we think you could soon pick up drumming, as you say you do tap-dancing and this will give you an idea of rhythm. Our season does not start until Whitsun, but there is quite a lot to do before, such as putting the Dining Room in order, checking the pots and cutlery, etc, so we should be glad if you could come along right away. We enclose our literature to give you an idea of the kind of place we have here and assure you that the chief characteristic of the camp is the friendly and homely atmosphere between staff and visitors. That is why we prefer to have girls who can join in with the fun and can help to keep things going on our dance nights.

Yvonne's father was a bit suspicious and rang the Town Clerk to check up on the place before letting her go. But he needn't have worried: Yvonne stayed for nineteen years and ended up a shareholder in the company.

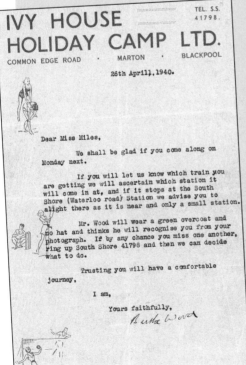

IVY HOUSE HOLIDAY CAMP LTD.
COMMON EDGE ROAD · MARTON · BLACKPOOL
TEL. S.S. 41798.

26th April, 1940.

Dear Miss Miles,

We shall be glad if you come along on Monday next.

If you will let us know which train you are getting we will ascertain which station it will come in at, and if it stops at the South Shore (Waterloo road) Station we advise you to alight there as it is near and only a small station.

Mr. Wood will wear a green overcoat and po hat and thinks he will recognise you from your photograph. If by any chance you miss one another, ring up South Shore 41798 and then we can decide what to do.

Trusting you will have a comfortable journey,

I am,

Yours faithfully,

Bertha Wood

Yvonne's instructions on how to recognise Fred at South Shore railway station. Apparently he wasn't there! The camp letterhead was designed and illustrated by Fred.

An early staff photograph – Fred (seated centre), flanked by myself and Yvonne, with Edna Ashby, a singer from Bolton (left) and Jenny Cardwell, a local helper in the kitchen (right).

Another staff photograph – Fred (seated centre), again flanked by myself and Yvonne, Corrine to my right and Annie, our cleaner to Yvonne's left. Jack, seated behind Fred and myself, returned to us after the war as a fully trained cook.

The 'artistes' – Yvonne (seated centre), flanked by Fred and another Jack, our pianist, with Corrine (right) and her friend Jane (left).

The staff girls

Most of the staff girls were employed on a seasonal basis. Jane Throup however also worked through the winter months painting the chalets and continued living at the camp even though her family had a house in Blackpool. She joined the staff in 1945 aged fifteen and recalls going to an audition with her older sister where they were expected to sing to Fred's piano accompaniment and perform dance routines. Jane was offered a job but her sister wasn't. At first she declined because of her lack of suitable clothes but Bertha soon put that right by giving her some of Corrine's. From that point on, Jane and Corrine became the best of friends.

Corrine and Jane in costume and (below) relaxing.

The 'Bird-Cage' or 'Scratching Pen', a converted hen house, provided dormitory accommodation for the staff girls.

More artistes, this time with the Amazons (standing).

favourites both with the campers and also at the local pub up the road, where they could drink, pint for pint, with the men and still arrive back to serve coffee in the show interval.

The weekly programme

Campers arrived on the Saturday afternoon. Immediately, a small committee was chosen from amongst them to agree the programme of activities for the week. The committee met in the house with Fred acting as an advisor. The strange thing was, although the members of the committee were sure that they had made the decisions for the programme, which I typed, it was exactly the same each week. So much for the diplomatic influence of the 'advisor'. The committee's other duties were to take the names of all the campers wishing to take part in the sports competitions, and to find anyone who was willing to do a turn or concoct a show in the

The Delvon Sisters

Yvonne was eventually joined at the camp by her younger sister Delmore, and later by their nieces Raquel and Kerena. When these Welsh girls got together Keith would complain that 'Half Wales' was in town. To earn extra money Yvonne and Delmore would sing elsewhere. The Delvon Sisters, as they were known, had regular bookings all over Lancashire. Yvonne also performed operatic arias and sometimes played the principal girl in winter pantomimes touring the north of England.

THE DELVON SISTERS

YVONNE   DELMORE
HARMONY IN MODERN STYLE

P.A.:— "HAYCLIFFE,"
50 LAYTON ROAD,
BLACKPOOL.
TEL. S.S. 41798

Fred and the Delvon Sisters.

'Harmony in Modern Style'.

Campers' Concert on the Friday night. They also had to nominate two or three people to note down any amusing things that occurred during the week. We called them the 'secret service'.

Things always got off to a great start on the Sunday night. This was when our own staff entertained the campers, beginning with the girls, dressed in short tops and long silk trousers which I made from yellow parachute silk, singing our 'Welcome' song composed by Fred. Our own two girls did turns in the show. Corrine sang 'You Made Me Love You' and also performed a song-and-dance act with her friend Jane, one of the staff girls; while Frankie, when still quite young, did an 'Isadora Duncan' extemporary dance which was very popular. Our pianist did a solo turn and Fred played the drums and did the compèring. There were also dances, such as the Valetta and Waltzes, and games such as 'Pass the Parcel'. The evening finished with a Conga which I led, on dry evenings, all around the camp. The show and dances created much fun and proved a good means of getting everyone acquainted and in a holiday mood.

Monday morning, and each subsequent day, started with Bing Crosby singing over the loud speaker 'Get Up, Get Up and

Fred, the master of ceremonies. People say he had a George Burns-like delivery, but unlike George he couldn't stop laughing at his own jokes. After welcoming the campers he would remind them of the camp rules, ending with the phrase, "Nobody to be out after lights-out – not officially anyway."

Meet the Sun Halfway', even if it was raining! Monday was the day the names of all those wishing to take part in the sports competitions were put in a hat and the opponents for the first round of games established. The games were then started and continued all through the week until the finals on Friday afternoon.

The Welcome song
Campers, campers, campers
Welcome to Ivy House Camp
We've got the blues on the ramp
Friends and neighbours are here in force
There's not a moment to be lost
This week is your holiday ...

The Sunday night shows were often themed;
Italian was a particular favourite ...

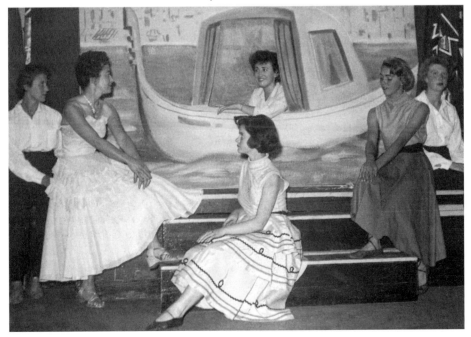

. . . as were our French shows.

Opposite above *Another favourite was 'The Gay Nineties'.*

Opposite below *Brenda Walsh had some theatrical training and was a specialist dancer. She was particularly fond of Keith and later became a Tiller girl.*

Ron at the drums.

The staff boys

Keith's friends, Les and Ron Firth, also played the drums at the camp shows. Fred used to pay Ron 10 shillings a week for two nights work, or 60 cigarettes. Ron invariably chose the cigarettes but the first thing Fred would do would be to 'caj' one off him. Bill Poole, who operated the spot light for the shows, never got paid at all!

Tea was taken early on Monday so that everyone could attend the Opera House Season Show at the Winter Gardens which started at 6 pm. Throughout the season we reserved 125 seats on the front three rows of the dress circle. Fred and I escorted the campers to their seats, staying for the show (we went so often

Group photographs of the campers and staff were taken on Monday mornings in front of Welcome Hall. Keith and his friends would often try to disrupt these photographs by getting in the way or even climbing on the roof of Welcome Hall!

More group photographs of campers and staff.

Opposite *The Opera House auditorium (above) and Empress Ballroom (below).*
The Winter Gardens also comprised the Planet Room, Palm Café, Galleon Bar,
Pavilion Theatre, Floral Hall, Renaissance Restaurant, Baronial Hall, Spanish Hall
and the Olympia Exhibition Hall
(courtesy of Blackpool Central Library).

Wednesday on the beach at South Shore.

that we could recite the patter off by heart), and then shepherded them into the Empress Ballroom where one of the big dance bands would be playing. When we were sure that everyone was settled, we took the opportunity to relax over a meal in the Renaissance Restaurant and later to dance to a four-piece band playing in the Baronial Hall. A quiet, enjoyable time after a hectic day.

Tuesday was an optional visit by coach to the Lake District, or a 'go as you please' day. Wednesday, if the weather was fit, Fred took a car-load of sandwiches and drinks for lunch on the beach at South Shore. Here, the sand was very firm and the campers were able to play cricket, run races or go riding. The sea came up twice a day, close enough to enable them to have a swim and there was a sloping area which was a good place for sunbathing. I had to have plenty of suntan lotion ready for when they all returned.

The Palace opened at the turn of the century as the Alhambra on a site adjoining the Tower Buildings. It had a Ballroom, an Italian Lounge and three Pleasure Pavilions with variety acts and films. The Theatre of Varieties could seat 2,800. It gave way to a department store development, a sign of changing times, in 1961 (courtesy of The Gazette, Blackpool).

Thursday was another early tea day as we had pre-booked seats at the Palace Theatre of Varieties where many famous comedians appeared over the years. Again, Fred and I accompanied the campers, escorting everyone to the Palace Ballroom at the end of the show, and leaving to have a quiet meal on our own.

Friday was mostly taken up with the finals of the sports competitions and rehearsals and preparations for the evening show and Campers' Concert. On Friday lunchtime the notes taken by the 'secret service' were handed to Fred, so that he could write a poem to be read during the evening, much to the embarrassment of the

*Staff often joined campers in the
tennis competition.*

*Campers rehearsing for the Friday
Concert.*

individuals concerned. This would always start with the words "This
is Fred reading Ivy House News. It has come to my attention …".
By late afternoon the competitions were finished and the names of
the winners given to Fred, again so that he could prepare speeches
for the prize-giving ceremony to come.

The evening events sometimes opened with a playlet, written by
Fred, performed by three campers (hero, heroine and villain). We
had the choice of two plays: one a melodramatic plot containing
lines like, "Get over to that wall, you silly little fool, or this gun
will go off"; the other, a sob story with a villainous landlord
saying, "You must pay the rent" and the heroine replying, "Oh no,
no, I cannot pay the rent." I had the job of typing the scripts.

But it was the Campers' Concert where the real 'talent'
lay. Regular campers came prepared, some with their
own music and comic patter. It was probably the
only time they had a captive audience! Some were

quite good and enjoyable, but others, like Ivy, had to be heard to be believed. She brought her own music but had the most appallingly tuneless voice. Every time Ivy was staying, Keith and his friends came to have a good laugh. They sat in a row in a corner with me in front of them to try to curtail their sniggering. Acts like this had to be applauded, but not too much in case they did an encore.

There was one hilarious turn where some of the men dressed up as women, complete with balloons, tights and high heels. Another incident stands out in the memory when a man was reciting with great gusto 'The Shooting of Dan McGrew'. When he came to the line, 'A shot rang out', his false teeth also shot out, straight across the floor towards a woman camper's chair. She jumped up with a scream. He simply walked over, put them back into his mouth and continued with the poem.

The evening finished with our 'Goodnight' song composed by Fred, the words being written on a large bed sheet held up so that everyone could sing along.

Saturday was the big clean-up to get the camp ready for the new arrivals later in the day, and the whole procedure began all over again.

It was hard work and sometimes I wondered if we would get through the whole season; but we made some good friends and had lots of letters of thanks and photographs of families. One I remember, sent personally to me, was from Albert, a grave digger

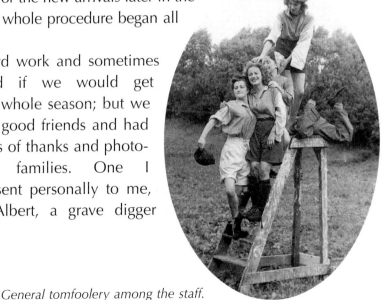

General tomfoolery among the staff.

Our 'Goodnight' song.

The 'Goodnight' song bed sheet seems to have found another use in this scene.

There was little time for rest and relaxation but to judge from these photographs, Yvonne and Jane seem to have made the most of it . . .

... and Fred too!

from Newcastle, who came to the camp every year. His card was a photograph of himself standing at the edge of a newly dug grave!

Out of season

At the end of the season when the staff girls went home, Yvonne stayed on to help me in the office. Letters of enquiry for accommodation for the forthcoming season amounted to hundreds a day, so there was a great deal of work to do. Yvonne sent out the camp brochure, whilst I concentrated on the bookings which followed. She was also

Working at the camp

Some of Frankie's earliest memories are of the Saturday clean-up. Aged five she helped strip the beds, count the bedding and get it ready to be sent off to the laundry. In the afternoon she was often the one to show the new arrivals to their chalets. In her teens she recalls working with the staff girls as a waitress and performer. Each waitress was responsible for waiting on 44 campers (thankfully it was a set menu so she didn't have to remember the orders!). After dinner the girls would clear away the tables and chairs to the side of the room and 'get glammed up' for the evening show, following which they had to move all furniture back again and lay the tables ready for breakfast.

Hi-de-Hi

Frankie also recalls Albert from Newcastle. He had a habit of painting his bare chest like a Red Indian, hiding and then jumping out to surprise other campers. He would also swing from the rafters of Welcome Hall imitating a monkey. His 'act' was certainly unusual and involved holding a dustbin lid handle between his teeth whilst executing somersaults. This trick he would rehearse all week along the bottom field, never leaving the camp, before the big performance on Friday night. He also did somersaults with a lighted cigarette in his mouth and a lighted cigarette the wrong way round in his mouth. After each somersault he would remove an item of clothing right down to his underpants. Apparently once, while performing his final somersault, he got his thumb stuck in his underpants and accidentally pulled them down to loud screams from the women in the audience!

a capable person to look after Frankie when she was growing up. Yvonne also developed a great admiration for Fred, which he 'lapped up'. Fred was very gullible where girls were concerned!

During the winter months we organised a 'Get-together' for the campers living in various parts of the country. Fred travelled to places such as Birmingham, Leeds and

A quiet moment with Yvonne.

Glasgow to organise these and so encourage future bookings. At home, the family would gather round the fire where Fred would make up interesting stories, sometimes serials which went on from evening to evening, and also anecdotes of his time in the army. He was an excellent story teller. We also read: first of all Enid Blyton's stories of the *Famous Five* progressing on to Arthur Ransome's *Swallows and Amazons*. Corrine and Keith loved these characters and when we went on a trip to the Lake District and stopped at White Moss, Keith got out of the car and quite seriously said, "I'll just have an egg sandwich and then go to find Octopus Lagoon". I remember hiring a rowing boat on Coniston and playing out Arthur Ransome's story, with some of us on the island warding off the others in the boat.

One of the campers, a seventeen year-old from Newcastle called John Smyth, had befriended Corrine. John was a keen musician and offered to relieve Fred and play the drums in our show. Out of season he and Corrine kept in touch by letter. When he came to stay again he brought his parents for a holiday. He later visited on weekend leaves from the army, staying in the house with us. On leaving the army John became one of our official drummers and Corrine's fiancé. They were married in May 1947.

Many of Keith's friends, like Ted Hinchcliffe, Ron Firth and Peter Beighton, spent a great deal of time at the camp taking advantage

John on holiday at the camp, flanked by his mother and another family member.

Corrine and John's wedding photographs were taken in the newly built camp garden. As coupons were still necessary to buy clothes, Corrine wore a suit.

of the sports facilities and generally getting up to no good. The camp also played host to Keith's football team, Ivy House Wanderers. Some of Keith's friends used to stay with us, especially Alan 'Cocky' Laycock whose mother had had to move to Bradford and to avoid disrupting Alan's schooling asked if we could take him in. Things like this just happened to us: we always seemed to be looking after someone else's children as well as our own.

Naughty boys

Ted and Alan recall Keith driving Fred's old Austin Seven saloon, now christened 'Ferdie', round the top field and on one occasion nearly reversing into a chalet. The boys would also try and hit golf balls from the putting green over the chalet roofs. "I don't know how many windows we broke" Ted confesses. There was trouble in the kitchen as well where the boys would wind up Jack by telling him that campers were complaining about his food, and then run away pursued by Jack wielding a carving knife. As Ron was doing a catering course, he would often get collared by Jack to help in the kitchen. Other attempts by Jack to illicit help from the boys, usually to clean or paint the swimming pool, would result in a mad dash to the opposite end of the camp.

Peter got into trouble regularly. He was so accident-prone that Bertha wouldn't let him in the house and would sometimes ban him from the camp for days on end. Stories about Peter are too numerous (and some potentially too embarrassing) to repeat here. Alan simply recalls, "Peter would stagger from one disaster to another. He was always falling over things and knocking things over, sometimes while in the process of apologising for some other misdemeanour". In his defence Peter considers his behaviour imaginative, if a little rash, and generally good natured and well intended. He does admit, however, to nearly circumcising Ted with a guillotine and almost burning down a church while collecting birds' eggs!

Keith, or 'Sam' to his friends, was always a keen footballer. As a youngster he played for South Shore Rovers FC.

Ivy House Wanderers Football Club

Ivy House Wanderers was started by Keith, with he and Alan as joint club secretaries. Keith was always the captain and according to Alan would never pass the ball. Alan played in goal. The team's initial strip was bright yellow, made from old parachute material by Mary, Jack's wife. They later played in blue and white when they joined the Blackpool Association of Boys Clubs Division II. The team was promoted in its first season but the league came to an end in 1952 with the call up for National Service. There was also a youth team, run by Ron, which played in the under–16 league. Peter also played in this team.

The home ground for Ivy House Wanderers was behind St Nicholas' church on Common Edge Road, with the 'Scratching Pen' doubling up as a changing room. Ted recalls trooping up the road from the camp to the pitch and afterwards sitting on the Aga cooker in the kitchen at Ivy House to dry off before being fed. Sometimes all eleven players would stay for a bath. Tommy Eccles remembers cycling to Ivy House all the way from Lytham to play football. When the team played away, usually at Stanley Park, Jack used to drive the boys to the games. To this day Tommy still doesn't know how all of them managed to cram into the back of the Humber Super Snipe shooting brake.

Ivy House Wanderers Football Club 1946, captained by Keith. Back row: J M Ogden, H M Reilly, A D Laycock, R J Moorhouse, G F Stone, A T Ogden. Front row: R P J Duffin, R M Joyce, J K Wood, A T Stevenson, C Eastwood.

Ivy House Wanderers Football Club 1949–50, managed by 'Jock' Courtney and still captained by Keith. Back row: Jack Vickers, Bob Joyce, 'Pop' Isles, Alan Whittam, Pete Fisher, Eric Taylor. Front row: 'Sam' Wood, 'Judd' Parkinson, Ted Hinchcliffe, Eddie Medcalf, Tommy Eccles. This team were winners of the Wentworth Cup and Champions of the Blackpool Association of Boys Clubs Division II.

The alternative 'ladies' football team, which also seems to have included John, on the practice pitch on the top field.

Frankie, meanwhile, was growing into a very vivacious little girl. Keith used to refer to her as 'The Great Little Miss'. From a very early age she had a natural bent towards free-style dancing. We took her to see *Swan Lake* at the Opera House and she came home and gave an almost perfect rendition of the 'Dance of the Little Swans'.

Frankie practising her ballet routine.

The gypsy caravans

The top field was always used as the site for permanent caravans but during the winter months several gypsy families would stay at the camp. Their caravans were positioned in the bottom field next to the chalets. Frankie recalls that the gypsies sometimes hired one or two of the chalets, decorating them inside with shocking pink satin fabric, and using them for parties and musical events.

An aerial photograph of the camp taken in March 1955, with the site covered in caravans (courtesy of English Heritage, NMR).

CHAPTER 6

Branching out

The move to self catering

Although the camp was reasonably successful, I realised when reviewing our bookings that only the middle two months of the season in any one year were completely full. This left the greater number of chalets empty for the early and late months – a great disadvantage and a dreadful waste of possible income.

We thought that we could utilise the chalets for a longer period if we offered self-catering facilities. This decided we set about transforming one of the blocks of four chalets. We provided a small cooker and designed a shelf unit for crockery, cutlery and food set behind a cupboard door which doubled as a fold-down table. Folding chairs completed the dining area, while a special bed designed to be raised up against the wall, created a reasonably sized living area.

The first season was a great success. All four self-catering chalets were fully booked all season greatly increasing our income at very little extra expense. We spent the following winter turning more chalets into self-service accommodation, but returning them to full board only for the central busy weeks, thus making good use of all the chalets for the whole season. Eventually we converted all the chalets into self-service and also built (using material from an old RAF hanger we acquired) a Rest Room, containing a café and shop, and a Games Room with table tennis and darts. It was also at this time that we abandoned our first swimming pool and constructed a new one on the site of the former camp garden.

Our second swimming pool.

The camp café and shop.

The 'Ivy Leaf Club'

Now that we no longer provided meals, the camp dining room, Welcome Hall, was superfluous. We therefore decided to convert it to a club, starting by transferring the bar from the Ivy House building and acquiring a full-size snooker table. We kept the stage for 'turns' from local talent and weekend shows. The Club was registered as the 'Ivy Leaf Club', with Fred as the owner and chairman, and we appointed a steward to attend to the details. It was open all the year round for local people as members and became a very popular retreat for the people on the Moss. The campers were automatically made members when they booked.

With the bar removed, we could now extend our own living quarters in Ivy House, creating a spacious lounge with a fire-place along the end wall. With a chintz-covered three-piece suite and curtains to match, a three-quarter mahogany grand piano, a large Dynotron radiogram and our original refectory table and

Our new lounge (courtesy of The Gazette, Blackpool).

chairs, it made quite an impressive room. Our original sitting room now became our dining room.

It was also about this time when the road outside Ivy House was widened to help alleviate increased traffic into Blackpool. Unfortunately, this meant we lost some of our garden and drive-way. Not to be outdone, we took advantage of the situation and built a petrol station!

Time off for painting

Fred and I could now afford to give ourselves one day off each week during the season. We usually drove into the Fylde countryside or to the more spectacular Lake District to find a spot with a delightful view for Fred to paint. Within an hour there would be a perfect watercolour

Standing in the porch, now only 3 feet from the roadside.

Fred sketching while the family relax.

sketch which he would later use as a 'cartoon' from which to create a larger watercolour painting. This he produced in a studio we built over our lounge, in place of the old hayloft. Painting was Fred's great passion: whenever there was a spare hour, the studio was where he would be.

Fred had always been a great admirer of the watercolour artist Percy Lancaster who was based not far away in Southport. Fred wrote to Percy and an invitation to visit his studio soon followed. There was an instant rapport between the two men. We in turn

Percy Lancaster

Percy Lancaster was born in Manchester in 1878. Originally trained as an architect, he soon turned to painting. He is best known as a watercolour painter and etcher recording everyday life in the English countryside, exhibiting widely including twenty times at the Royal Academy. He was elected a member of the Royal Society of British Artists in 1914 and of the Royal Institute of Painters in Watercolours in 1921. He died in Southport in 1951.[40]

Two of Fred's watercolours, painted in 1948: one of a typical Fylde farmstead;
the other a view of the Old Man of Coniston.

Paintings by Percy Lancaster and Fred on the walls of our dining room (courtesy of The Gazette, Blackpool).

Painting next to our Bentley. This was my favourite car which we bought second-hand in the late 1950s. Fred later traded it in for a large blue-and-white monstrosity in the shape of a Chevrolet, looking like a mobile aircraft carrier, with prominent pointed fins and a sliding roof. I don't think I ever forgave him for that.

invited Percy and his friend 'Cinders' for a stay in Blackpool, which they accepted. We spent several days showing them round the Fylde and later touring around the Lake District. Fred and Percy painted together, Percy making pithy remarks about Fred's sketches. I remember one piece of advice was "Put more guts in it, Laddie."

One day at Ullswater Fred set himself up at the lakeside and started a picture. I looked across the lake at the distant fells and thought I would like to be able to draw them too. I rummaged about amongst his painting gear in the car and found a small sketch pad and pencil, sat on the edge of the road and started to put down on paper what I could see. When Fred had finished I showed him what I had done. He said, "Well you've got the shapes all right, but one doesn't put in every little stone and tuft of grass!" This was my first lesson in drawing from nature and I was quite surprised at the result.

Due to our regular bookings for the Opera House, Fred became

In the studio. Fred and Elaine Smith, the first Miss Blackpool in 1954, with her portrait. (courtesy of The Gazette, Blackpool).

Fred continued to be a keen photographer. These, taken in the early 1950s, are some of many photographic portraits of Corrine, Keith and Frankie.

very friendly with the manager of the theatre. As a result Fred was invited to paint a portrait of the star of the show each season. The star, usually a famous and popular girl singer, would come to the house for sittings in the studio. The portrait was then exhibited by the local art society before being given to the star to take home at the end of the season. The stars included the likes of Eve Boswell, Joan Reagan, Sabrina, Yana, Sheila Buxton, Lynne Kennington, Ruby Murray, Rosemary

Squires, Kathy Kirby, Alma Cogan and Mary Hopkin. Fred was also on the panel of judges for the annual Miss Blackpool Beauty Contest, and a portrait was part of the prize for the winner. He even painted Ann Sidney, the then Miss World.

Fred had his own definition of beauty, "Wide-set eyes, a short nose, sharp chin, and lustrous hair. The eyes, when studied from the artist's point of view, should form a perfect triangle with the tip of the nose."

Fire in the Club

One winter's morning I was awakened by calls up the stairs, "There's smoke in the bar". It was the Club cleaner. Only the barman and steward had keys to the bar itself, so we could not get in. I rang the fire brigade who arrived promptly, but could not raise the barman. (We later learned that he was actually on the camp, visiting friends in one of the caravans, and completely oblivious to what was going on.)

We started to drag the tables and chairs away from the bar to clear a space for the firemen, until the smoke be came too over-powering. Curiously, although the front door on the west side of the Club was open, the firemen went round the back of the building, where there was a high wind blowing, and proceeded to smash all the windows. This of course let in the wind which immediately caught the flames with a huge 'whoosh' and set the ceiling ablaze. "Why ever did they go to the east side, with that wind blowing" asked Fred, as he viewed the scene with dismay.

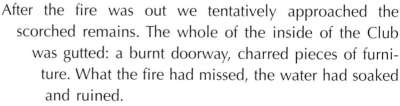

After the fire was out we tentatively approached the scorched remains. The whole of the inside of the Club was gutted: a burnt doorway, charred pieces of furniture. What the fire had missed, the water had soaked and ruined.

The law requires licensees to keep bars open, so we set about clearing everything up and making a temporary bar in order to continue to serve drinks. Brushes, shovels, scrapers and garden rakes were all used to get the debris cleared. With odds and ends of chairs from the house and some of the members and a fresh supply of drinks and glasses delivered, a small oasis was created amongst the general scene of devastation.

The real task began the next morning. The skeleton of the building was still there but the entire wall linings needed replacing, and the ceiling, of course, had to be rebuilt. The members were marvellous, rallying round to help with the building operations. "We are all here, Gov" said one, "Just tell us what to do", and with Fred acting as foreman, planning the order of work and giving each man his special job, the place was soon a noisy hive of industry. The make-shift bar was opened at the usual hour, each evening, when it was 'down tools' and by the end of the week we were ready to get a joiner in to rebuild the bar properly. In what seemed like no time at all, the Club was back up and running.

To celebrate, we had a big re-opening party, with the Firth brothers, Les and Ron (Keith's friends and excellent caterers), doing a fabulous buffet. The actress Violet Carson performed the re-opening ceremony. She was a colleague of Fred's on the Miss Blackpool panel of judges. Fred also invited four of the Misses Blackpool to add a bit of glamour and help serve the food.

Ilkley

After the war we had money to invest from the sale of our Red Court hotel, so when we saw an advert offering a 'Spa' hotel in Ilkley, at a very reasonable price, we were definitely interested.

We drove over to investigate. 'Marlborough House' proved to be a very impressive detached stone-built Victorian hotel, standing in its own grounds, with a tennis court along one side and a putting green along the other. Entering by the central front door we found a square hall with a decorated hand-basin with ornamental tap, supplying Ilkley Mineral 'Spa' Water. A door off the hall led to a most magnificent room running the full width of the double-fronted building. The floor was polished oak and the windows, which occupied the whole of the back wall, were of the Gothic Revival style, giving a breathtaking panoramic view over Blubberhouses Moor.

Upstairs were spacious bedrooms; enough to accommodate about thirty people. The bathroom was a period piece, with a high iron bath with a canopy over, a blue floral-patterned hand-basin and toilet, and a black-and-white tiled floor. In the basement were a self-contained, owner-occupier flat, a large catering kitchen and staff dining room.

At the time Billie and Muriel were finding it difficult to generate enough income from their grocery shop for their expanding family. We asked them, if we bought Marlborough House, would they be prepared to manage it, with Billie as cook and Muriel as house-keeper. After they had seen it they agreed, so we went ahead and bought the hotel and began the necessary works to smarten it up to receive the first visitors. We placed an advert in the Sunday news-papers offering accommodation in the Yorkshire Dales for people wanting to take touring or walking holidays.

The response was not up to our expectations. However, a few local people started asking if they could live there as residents. We therefore began accepting permanent boards. After a year or two all the rooms were taken on this basis, with residents bring-ing their own furniture to create a comfortable living place, and all meals provided in a communal dining room. Even Fred and Billie's father decided to move there.

Most of the residents were retired but I remember one man with a business in Leeds who was collected every weekday morning in a chauffeur-driven Daimler. The car would draw up at the front door and out would step 'Dunbar', the chauffeur, who would go upstairs to collect his master's briefcase and ceremoniously carry it into the car!

Bowness

Following Corrine and John's marriage, we bought a run-down missionary hotel in Bowness-on-Windermere with the idea that it would be a living for Corrine and John and a possible haven for us.

Oak Bank Hotel, Bowness-on-Windermere.

A pencil drawing by Percy Lancaster of the rooftops of Bowness-on-Windermere, viewed from the garden at Oak Bank. We used to stay with Corrine and John when travelling with Percy.

'Oak Bank', as the hotel was called, was a three-storey building occupying a prominent position in the town with views down to the lake. It comprised a good sized dining room with two reception rooms, and upstairs sleeping accommodation for 36 people. To the rear were the family living quarters and hotel kitchen.

At first Corrine and John had a pretty thin time, but after about two years the hotel featured in the *Good Food Guide*. This was

Johnny on a visit to the camp.

remarkable as Corrine's only experience of cooking had been helping us serve food at the camp.

After about three years, a plaintive call on the 'phone, "Mummy I'm pregnant, and very sick". 'Mummy' left the camp to go to the rescue and stayed to do the cooking and Fred came up once a week with the Ivy House Books for me to keep up to date. So, eventually, our first grandchild was born: Johnny.

A few years later, they had another son: Martin. By this time Corrine and John had taken over the ownership of Oak Bank from us, and had converted the bedrooms to self-catering accommodation in much the same way as we had done in the camp chalets.

Keith and Elizabeth at Ivy House in 1958 . . .

A family of painters

Like Fred, Keith had developed a keen interest in painting. He studied fine art at Blackpool College of Art and gained his art teaching qualifications at Leeds College of Art, followed by National Service in the RAF. While at Leeds he met fellow art student Elizabeth Theakstone. They were married in Bradford in August 1955, the Wood contingent staying at Marlborough House the night before the wedding. They soon set up home in Accrington, close to where both were teaching.

Two years later an opportunity arose back in Blackpool at the Grundy House Museum and Art Gallery. A curator was needed to arrange art

... and later with their two boys Jason and Crispin.

exhibitions and manage a collection of antiquities from the Blackpool and Fylde area. Keith and Elizabeth took the post and they moved into the apartment above the ground-floor museum. They also became part-time lecturers at Blackpool College of Art, Elizabeth taking over as sole curator when Keith became a full-time lecturer. They had two sons: the first, Jason, shortly after moving to Blackpool; and the second, Crispin, three years later.

Having left school, Frankie's first idea was to take a secretarial course so that she would be able to take over from me in the camp office. However, with a little persuasion from Fred, she chose instead to enrol on the graphic design course at Blackpool College of Art. Keith was already teaching there and I had enrolled myself on a non-

Frankie and Whit's wedding party at Ivy House in August 1959.

vocational course in painting. It was here that Frankie met fellow student, David Whitaker, known simply as 'Whit' as there were so many 'Davids' at the College at the time.

Whit left the College early to take up the offer of a job as a commercial artist in London. He kept in touch with Frankie by hitching a lift every weekend to Blackpool, but in the end this proved too exhausting. After a holiday together, staying with Corrine in the Lake District, they decided to get married and live near his work.

Whit eventually went on to complete his art

The Whitaker boys, Timothy, Simon and Joe, with Frankie.

education at the Royal Academy School of Art in London and then secured part-time teaching in three different art colleges at Brighton, Wimbledon and Ruskin College, Oxford, later becoming a full-time lecturer at Wimbledon. During this time they had three sons, Timothy, Simon and Joe. When Frankie rang us from hospital to tell us the news about Joe, she spoke to Fred and said, "I'm sorry Daddy, but it's another boy!" Fred had expected a little girl, even sending Frankie pink clothes for the baby in anticipation. Joe was our seventh grandson.

CHAPTER 7

Into retirement

Selling up

By the mid-1960s Fred and I decided we had worked long enough. The chalets required refurbishment and we didn't think that, at our age, we would be able to recoup the money needed for the job. We put an advert in the local paper: 'For Sale, Small Holiday Camp', giving only a 'phone number but no details of where it was situated. We hoped the sale would be an attractive proposition as besides the camp itself we were offering a licence for twelve permanent, 22-foot caravans; a petrol station on the main road into and out of Blackpool; and the licence for the Club.

Early on the morning after publication, a Mr Wilmot arrived asking if this was the camp for sale. He had passed it regularly and surmised that it must be the one. What attracted him most (he told us later) were the 'One Arm Bandits' in the Club. (Apparently the income from these was impossible for the tax man to trace.) He decided, on the spot, to buy and within a month he was the new owner. We were to keep the house and adjacent garden and patio.

Mr Wilmot soon set about rebuilding the chalets, the Club and the swimming pool. He also renamed the camp 'Ivy House Holiday Centre'.

Opposite above *The new chalets built by Mr Wilmot.*

Opposite below *Our garden.*

Holidays abroad

In the winters we went abroad for the warmth and sunshine, taking three separate months in different places. One favourite place was Torremolinos in Spain, then a charming fishing village, with one very exclusive hotel and one more modest one, The Eden, where we stayed. Fred did some delightful sketches of the narrow winding road, lined by red-roofed cottages and leading to the sea, which we could see from our balcony.

On another occasion we went with a private party to Florida, chartering a 'plane. We stayed in a very luxurious hotel on the front at Miami Beach. During our stay we were offered and bought a piece of land in what we were told was planned to be a yachting complex. It seemed a good investment at the time but I think they saw us coming. The land is now under water!

Fred's deteriorating health

Throughout his life Fred had smoked cigarettes, but following breathing troubles he was advised by his doctor to give up. The doctor, a personal friend, told him that cigars or pipe tobacco would be OK, so Fred said "If you give me a prescription for cigars, I'll smoke those." Needless to say, this was not forthcoming; but from then on Fred smoked cigars during the day, and a pipe in the evenings when he was relaxing.

Fred, with his pipe, on his swing seat where he loved to sit in the sun.

Fred and I relaxing in the lounge.

One day Fred was upstairs in his studio when I heard the sound of something heavy falling. I went fearfully up to see what had happened. Fred was lying on the floor and couldn't get up. Apparently he had broken a small bone at the base of his spine and couldn't walk. After several weeks, things were no better and eventually our doctor called in a specialist who made a thorough examination. Fred had developed cancer.

I quickly arranged for a bed at Northwood Nursing Home, North Shore. After a short time, Fred was taken to Victoria Hospital to the special cancer unit. There I met the specialist. I said "Well, what's the verdict?" He replied, very abruptly, "A month," and walked on. I was stunned, and it took all my self control to hide my feelings when Fred came out. He went back to the nursing home but it wasn't long before the end came. It was one evening when we were preparing tea. The 'phone rang and I answered. An agitated voice said "Is that Dr Fridgeon?" (our doctor). When I said "No", she gabbled different names, all of which were connected with Fred's illness, so I said "I think it's me you want, Mrs Wood." She then said what I was now expecting, "Mr Wood has died". He was aged 80.

Leaving Ivy House

Fred died in February 1980. I continued to live at Ivy House for a further three years, cooking in a kitchen which had catered for 125 people, plus family and staff. I could still hear the familiar sounds of the Club next door and see the holiday-makers arriving in the summer, but as winter approached and there were no holiday-makers around, I began to feel rather vulnerable.

Ivy House was detached and well away from any other houses but close enough, since road widening, to the pavement to be a target for passing youths. In fact, one night one of a party of young men, having obviously spent too much time in the local pub along the road, casually kicked in the bottom of the glass front door. As I was now sleeping downstairs, this was very frightening.

Very reluctantly, after 48 years at Ivy House, I decided I would be better living in a smaller place and if possible with other people around.

Epilogue

Bertha left Ivy House in 1983, aged 78 and moved to a flat over-looking Highfield Road Park in South Shore. By chance, the mother and aunts of one of her new neighbours had worked at Cobden Mill in Bolton where her father had been manager.

Mr Wilmot's Ivy House Holiday Centre went through a quick succession of new owners but by the late 1980s both it and Ivy House had fallen into disrepair. Interestingly, Jack Chamberlain was retained as an employee right to the end. By 1991, the whole area, including Ivy House, had been cleared for redevelopment. A small housing estate called Belverdale Gardens now occupies the site.

Within a few years Bertha moved to live in Windermere to be

Bertha at home in Windermere.

nearer Corrine and John and also Keith and Elizabeth, who had retired there from Blackpool. As she hints in her Memoirs, Fred and Bertha had always had a desire to live in the Lake District. At first she lived in a flat in Fairfield Road, but later decided, when aged 88, to take up the offer of a room at Nine Oaks, the local Abbeyfield Home.

Throughout the last twenty years Bertha has kept herself active and engaged in a variety of different areas, from membership of art societies through to participation in university summers schools and distance learning courses. Her hope, as the last line of her Memoirs says, is to 'carry on being interested in what is occurring in the outside world and, if possible, take some part in it.'

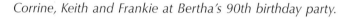

Corrine, Keith and Frankie at Bertha's 90th birthday party.

The 'Magnificent Seven' grandsons at Bertha's 90th birthday party – the first get together since the Ivy House days.

Although Bertha remains in relatively good health, she has had to bear the loss of two of her three of her children. Corrine died in July 2002 and Keith one year later. Earlier, in March 1995, her son-in-law John had died.

The family enterprise and innovative spirit lives on, however, in Bertha's seven grandsons and their various offspring, though curiously none of them have shown any inclination to go into the holiday camp industry.

Notes

1. J. K. Walton, *Lancashire: A Social History, 1558–1939* (Manchester University Press, 1987), chapter 13.
2. J. K. Walton, *Blackpool* (Edinburgh University Press, 1998), chapters 4–5.
3. M. P. Fogarty, *Prospects of the Industrial Areas of Great Britain* (London: Methuen, 1945), p. 218.
4. Roy Fuller, *Souvenirs* (London: London Magazine Editions, 1980).
5. Alan Fowler, *Lancashire Cotton Operatives and Work, 1900–1950* (Aldershot: Ashgate, 2003), pp. 132–41.
6. Mike Savage, *The Dynamics of Working-class Politics* (Cambridge University Press, 1987).
7. Fowler, *Lancashire Cotton Operatives*, pp. 44–5, 87.
8. Fogarty, *Prospects*, p. 218.
9. Ibid., p. 214.
10. P. Harris, 'Social leadership and social attitudes in Bolton, 1919–1939', Ph.D. thesis, Lancaster University, 1973, chapters 1, 6; Walton, *Lancashire*, p. 348.
11. Fowler, *Lancashire Cotton Operatives*, pp. 77–9.
12. William Woodruff, *The Road to Nab End* (London: Abacus, 2000).
13. Fogarty, *Prospects*, pp. 212–14.
14. Fowler, *Lancashire Cotton Operatives*, p. 71.
15. Harold Palmer, *Not a Sparrow Falls* (Preston: Winckley, 1988).
16. Walton, *Blackpool*, pp. 117–18.
17. J. K. Walton, 'The seaside resorts of England and Wales, 1900–1950', in G. Shaw and A. Williams (eds), *The Rise and Fall of British Coastal Resorts* (London: Mansell, 1997), pp. 26–31.
18. Charles Graves, *– And the Greeks* (London: Geoffrey Bles, 1930), pp. 187–91.
19. Gary Cross (ed.), *Worktowners at Blackpool* (London: Routledge, 1990); Gary Cross and John K. Walton, *The Playful Crowd: Pleasure Places in the Twentieth Century* (New York: Columbia University Press, forthcoming

2005), chapter 3; *Daily Dispatch*, 3–7 August 1934. For William Holt himself, see his autobiography *I Haven't Unpacked* (London: G. G. Harrap, 1939).

20. J. K. Walton, *The British Seaside: Holidays and Resorts in the Twentieth Century* (Manchester University Press, 2000), chapter 4.

21. Walton, *Blackpool*, chapter 5.

22. Walton, 'Seaside resorts of England and Wales', pp. 31–4; J. K. Walton, *The Blackpool Landlady* (Manchester University Press, 1978), chapter 9; S. Barton, *Working-class Organisations and Popular Tourism, 1840–1970* (Manchester University Press, 2005), chapter 6; Colin Ward and Dennis Hardy, *Goodnight Campers! The History of the British Holiday Camp* (London: Mansell, 1986).

23. Walton, *Blackpool Landlady*, chapters 4–7.

24. *Daily Dispatch*, 6 August 1934.

25. *British Railways Holiday Guide*, Wales and North-West England, 1952, p. 154.

26. *United Kingdom Holiday Guide*, 1939, p. 82.

27. Ward Lock & Co., *Red Guide to Blackpool* (n.d., c. 1959), p. 16.

28. Harvey Taylor, *A Claim on the Countryside* (Keele University Press, 1997).

29. For these ideas, see J. K. Walton, *Tourism, Fishing and Redevelopment: Post-war Whitby, 1945–1970*, University of Cambridge: Institute of Continuing Education, Occasional Paper No. 5, 2005.

30. For this theme, see Cross, *Worktowners at Blackpool*.

31. For Butlin, see especially Ward and Hardy, *Goodnight Campers!*

32. Walton, *Blackpool Landlady*, chapter 3; Sam Davies and Bob Morley (eds), *County Borough Election Results, 1919–1938*, vol. 1 (Aldershot: Ashgate, 1999), 'Blackpool'.

33. John Golley, *Genesis of the Jet: Frank Whittle and the Invention of the Jet Engine* (Shrewsbury: Airlife, 1997), chapter 1.

34. For a full description and photograph, see **www.imagesofengland.org.uk**.

35. For vernacular building materials and construction techniques, see Richard C. Watson and Marion E. McClintock, *Traditional Houses of the Fylde* (University of Lancaster: Centre for North-West Regional Studies, Occasional Paper No. 6, 1979). For full descriptions and photographs of the listed buildings, see **www.imagesofengland.org.uk**.

36. Kathleen Eyre, *Seven Golden Miles: The Fantastic Story of Blackpool* (Clapham: Dalesman, 1975), pp. 161–2.

37. Ward and Hardy, *Goodnight Campers!*, pp. 60–3; Walton, *The British*

Seaside, pp. 129–30; see also **www.butlinsmemories.com** and **www.images-ofengland.org.uk** for a full description and photograph of the listed building.

38. For this theme, see Dennis Hardy and Colin Ward, *Arcadia for All: The Legacy of a Makeshift Landscape* (London: Mansell, 1984).

39. For this theme, see Jeffrey Richards, *The Age of the Dream Palace: Cinema and Society in Britain, 1930–1939* (London: Routledge & Kegan Paul, 1984).

40. For further information, see Huon L. Mallalieu, *The Dictionary of British Watercolour Artists up to 1920* (Woodbridge, 1976).